Cost-Effective Training

The Kogan Page Practical Trainer Series

Series Editor: Roger Buckley

PRACTICAL ATA TRAINER SERIES

Cost-Effective Training

A Manager's Guide

TONY NEWBY

KOGAN PAGE
Published in association with the
Institute of Training and Development

First published in1992

Apart from any fair dealing for the purposes of research or private study, or criticism or review, as permitted under the Copyright, Designs and Patents Act, 1988, this publication may only be reproduced, stored or transmitted, in any form or by any means, with the prior permission in writing of the publishers, or in the case of reprographic reproduction in accordance with the terms of licences issued by the Copyright Licensing Agency. Enquiries concerning reproduction outside those terms should be sent to the publishers at the undermentioned address:

Kogan Page Limited
120 Pentonville Road
London N1 9JN

© Tony Newby, 1992

British Library Cataloguing in Publication Data

A CIP record of this book is available from the British Library.

ISBN 0 7494 0552 X

Typeset by Koinonia Ltd, Bury
Printed and bound in Great Britain by Biddles Ltd, Guildford and King's Lynn

Contents

Series Editor's Foreword

Organizations get things done when people do their jobs effectively. To make this happen they need to be well trained. A number of people are likely to be involved in this training: identifying the needs of the organization and of the individual, selecting or designing appropriate training to meet those needs, delivering it and assessing how effective it was. It is not only 'professional' or full-time trainers who are involved in this process; personnel managers, line managers, supervisors and job holders are all likely to have a part to play.

This series has been written for all those who get involved with training in some way or another whether they are senior personnel managers trying to link the goals of the organization with training needs or job holders who have been given responsibility for training newcomers. Therefore, the series is essentially a practical one which focuses on specific aspects of the training function. This is not to say that the theoretical underpinnings of the practical aspects of training are unimportant. Anyone seriously interested in training is strongly encouraged to look beyond 'what to do' and 'how to do it' and to delve into the areas of why things are done in a particular way.

The authors have been selected because they have considerable practical experience. All have shared, at some time, the same difficulties, frustrations and satisfactions of being involved in training and are now in a position to share with others some helpful and practical guidelines.

Over recent years line managers have taken to heart the message that training should be regarded as an investment rather than a cost. Having done so it is only to be expected that they would wish to know what the return is on their investment. In this book Tony Newby shows managers how to ensure that training in their organizations is effective in addressing real performance problems and value for money by outlining how aspects of that return can be measured. Once the costs of training have been calculated in financial terms the returns can be assessed in terms of the quality and effectiveness of the training that is delivered. Quality can be looked at in terms of the proper application of a systematic approach to training and effectiveness by measuring the impact of training on work behaviour and the cost benefits of that training.

The book is of value to all trainers who have to respond to the question 'How do I know that I've got my money's worth?' and it is of specific value to those line managers with little experience of training who have to take on a training role as part of their line function. It is also of interest to those trainers and managers who believe in the value of a collaborative partnership between line management and trainers and who need practical tips on how to establish such a partnership.

ROGER BUCKLEY

Introduction: The 'Informal Trainer'

A large amount of job-related training occurs in organizations where either there is no professional trainer or only a training administrator who deals with external course bookings and the like. However, the absence of a person with the formal title of 'trainer' does not mean that there is no training taking place, nor does it make it any less important that the question of value for money, or cost-effectiveness, of training be addressed.

Much training is carried out in a relatively informal, usually well-intentioned but sometimes haphazard way, by line and sales managers, supervisors, computer specialists, accountants, etc. In terms of numbers, there are very many more managers and supervisors than professional trainers, and there are few managers who do not have some element of training responsibility in their job. Even when managers do not directly deliver training, they have a key role in choosing training purchases, briefing trainers and ensuring that what has been learned through training subsequently gets used in the workplace. This book addresses the needs of these 'informal trainers' with practical guidance on how they can get the greatest learning results in the most cost-effective manner from the effort that they and their colleagues put into training.

Is this Book for You?

This is designed to be a practical 'how to do it' book. It spells out in clear, step-by-step fashion how cost-effective training can be achieved through measures that range from linking training into corporate strategy to measuring the pay-offs from training outputs.

The book is written for people at the sharp end of organizations, whether private or public sector, and avoids academic debate. It is intended to be a comprehensive and self-contained guide and therefore does not send you chasing off to find other books or obscure articles listed in footnotes.

How to Use this Book

Each chapter begins with an outline summary. As well as the explanatory text, often broken down into precise instructions on how to carry out particular tasks, you will find various exercises, checklists and quizzes which are labelled 'Activities'. These are provided to help you to relate the book content to your own organizational situation. There are also a number of sections headed 'Practical Tips' which offer ideas for increasing cost-effectiveness in training.

Chapter 1 discusses the purposes of training in organizations and asks 'Is training worth doing?'. It discusses the balance of quality versus quantity in training provision and draws the key linkage between corporate strategy and training. What is (and what is not) a training need is explained and the connections between skill acquisition, motivation and personality are clarified. The reader can start to develop a personal plan of action based upon this book.

In Chapter 2, the corporate context within which training takes place is examined. A marketing-led approach to training is advocated. The importance of corporate commitment to training is reviewed and the influences on cost-effectiveness that are exerted by the training infrastructure are described.

Chapter 3 focuses upon design issues which make for effective training. It provides a comprehensive overview of the training cycle: diagnostics, design, delivery and evaluation.

In Part 1 of Chapter 4, methods to develop a collaborative working partnership between managers and trainers are presented. In Part 2, guidelines are given for buying-in training services and employing consultants, in particular addressing the question: 'How do you ensure that you get what you ask for?'

Practical guidance for the 'part-time' trainer is offered in Chapter 5, with descriptions of when and how to use a number of training techniques. It also describes some of the basic principles of learning that apply to all training, whether formalized in the classroom or in those informal opportunities such as the regular staff meeting, 'corridor counselling', the kerbside conference, or the corporate conference.

Finally, in Chapter 6, measurement of training results – in terms both of its impact on work behaviour and on profitability – is considered. Why end-of-course 'happy sheets' are inadequate is explained and better alternatives are described. Guidance is offered on the creation of an organizational framework that will support systematic assessment of training effectiveness.

The range of techniques available for measuring effectiveness is outlined and the timing of training assessments is discussed. An Appendix to the chapter offers several outline structures for workshops to assist with learning the skills of measuring training effectiveness.

1 What is Training For?

$\triangleright$ SUMMARY $\triangleleft$

This chapter discusses the purposes of training in organizations and asks, 'Is training worth doing?'. It discusses the balance of quality versus quantity in training provision. The links are illustrated between corporate strategy and training. What is (and what is not) a training need is explained, and the connections between skill acquisition, motivation and personality are clarified. The reader can start to develop a personal plan of action based upon this book.

Introduction

You may be someone who buys in training for your organization or you may yourself be directly involved in design or delivery of training. You may not be directly involved in training, but perhaps have the responsibility of monitoring the performance of whoever does those tasks. Whichever group you belong to, this book has one overall aim: to help you achieve value for money from all training with which you are involved.

So what do I mean by 'training'? It certainly includes the conventional 'course', run either as a public event or in-house. But a definition of training also extends to such activities as:

- kerbside conferences and other coaching opportunities;
- training elements within regular staff meetings;
- distance learning;
- open learning;

- corporate communications events;
- problem-solving teams or 'action learning';
- computer-based training (CBT);
- interactive video.

Any activity intended to improve people's capability to perform a work task by means of improving their skills or increasing their knowledge is 'training'. (By the way, throughout this book I shall use words such as 'trainee', 'participant' and 'course member' to provide variety in the way that I describe the people who are on the receiving end of training; however, there is no implication in my use of a word such as 'trainee' that this person is a beginner or new entrant to the organization.)

One of the principles of effective training is that people learn better if they have some idea of what to expect during the training process and some personal investment in achieving the goals that the training addresses. This is a principle you may like to use for yourself, here and now.

ACTIVITY

Take about five minutes to browse through the Contents list at the start of this book and, if you like, also the Index at the back. Reflect on your reasons for reading this book. What do you hope to get out of it? How are you going to justify (even if only to yourself) the investment of time and mental energy that it calls for? Make a note of your answers to the statements and questions below on a separate sheet of paper. (These do not have to be final and definitive answers – as you go through the book, other things may become significant for you.)

What I hope to learn from this book:

How many hours am I likely to invest in reading and thinking about these matters?

What is that investment worth? (Salary cost/opportunity cost/loss of leisure time/whatever.)

The fact that you are reading this book suggests:

- that you think training should make a positive difference to the way your organization works (but currently you are unsure whether it is doing so);
- that (probably) you have experienced training that left you feeling dissatisfied, typically because of one or more of the following reasons:

- the purpose was unclear
- the stated aims were not achieved
- the content failed to relate to participants' own experience
- the approach was academic rather than practical
- the classroom learning failed to survive the transfer back into the workplace
- it was difficult to measure benefits from the training
- that you have a responsibility for achieving results and believe that *effective* training might more than pay for itself.

Quality versus Quantity of Training

You may have a concern that this book will demand of you far more training than your organization can reasonably sustain. It will not! Quality rather than quantity has to be the goal if you want to see cost-effective training: the cost-effective approach is to do less, not more, training but to ensure that it is accurately targeted, efficiently delivered and that it is put to use.

Getting it right (preferably, right first time) depends upon having a thought-through training strategy. It also depends upon accurate identification of what needs to change (and recognition of which parts training can tackle and which parts require non-training measures). 'Quality' also requires you to understand what makes the difference between well-designed and poorly designed training and what helps or hinders people from using new knowledge and skills when they return to their jobs.

There are two basic rules that should shape all your decisions about training, whatever kind of organization you work in – commercial, public sector or charitable.

PRACTICAL TIPS

Rule 1: never train unless you can clearly identify the results –
'Anything else is wishful thinking'.

Rule 2: Only train for things that will make the organization run better –
'Nice-to-Know is not the same as Need-to-Know'.

'Learning for learning's sake' may have its justifications; but those justifications do not extend to helping organizations to operate more effectively or efficiently. It is a fundamental idea in this book that training only makes sense within the context of the purposes for which an organization exists. Purposeful activity is not, of course, the exclusive preserve of commerce and industry.

Another fundamental idea running throughout is that, if you cannot tell what difference the training is making, it is not worth doing it. How to make training effective – and then measure that effectiveness – will be described in later chapters.

Your Personal Action Plan

In keeping with the practical focus of this book, you may also like to develop a personal action plan that makes use of the ideas it describes. A common design failing in training is that 'action planning' is something tacked onto the end of a course (or tucked away in the final chapter of a book). The consequence is that action plans are completed by people in a rush to get away; psychologically, the course (or book) is already finished. When such plans are completed, they often amount to 'going through the motions', containing over-ambitious statements that the individual does not expect to implement. Furthermore, end-of-course action planning can easily result in good ideas that occurred during a course being lost sight of ('What was it they said on Tuesday morning...?').

An ongoing action plan makes this kind of problem much less likely. It also encourages you continually to ask yourself: 'What use can I make of what I am reading here?' As you read through the book make a note of any ideas that strike you as potentially useful in your own situation. Why not prepare an 'Ideas Diary' on a sheet of paper as a draft action plan made up of such notes; there will be other activities, checklists and the like for you to work with throughout the book.

Is Training Worth the Bother?

Where quality standards in training are low – and its effects consequently small, unpredictable or unmeasurable – expectations also tend to be low. The perception is that training really does not matter. Outbreaks of faddishness ('flavour-of-the-month training') also reinforce the idea that it is not a significant contributor to organizational effectiveness; that – at best – 'training will do no harm'. However, there are more systematic ways to judge whether or not training matters.

One method is to calculate what training costs the organization: how much is training taking off the gross profit line, and how much is it adding back? Training incurs direct costs: the money, time and expertise required to design and run training events; the pay and overheads of course members. It also imposes indirect costs in the form of training premises and administration. In addition, there are the opportunity costs of training, for the organization as a whole or within the training operation. At the macro-level money spent on training might instead be invested in, say, capital goods; operatives could be delivering goods or services instead of sitting in a training room. Within the training budget, money spent on, say, a senior manager attending a prestige business school course might leave no money for on-the-job induction training.

The checklist that follows will help you to calculate costs presently being incurred. Ask yourself whether these should be thought of as 'costs' or 'investments'.

ACTIVITY *Checklist to review the cost of training*		
MAJOR CATEGORY OF COST	**ITEM**	**ESTIMATED COST**

Fixed capital	Premises
	Furniture and fixed equipment
	   (eg, wallboards)
	Wired services (eg, CCTV, computer links)
	Training equipment (audio-visual, tools,
	   machinery, word processors, etc)
	Resources (eg, training packages, computer
	   programs, purchased videos, books)
	Motor vehicles	

	SUB-TOTAL	
Working capital	Maintenance and repair of equipment Consumables (eg, stationery, floppy disks) Materials used in the course of training	
	SUB-TOTAL	

MAJOR CATEGORY OF COST	ITEM	ESTIMATED COST
Personnel/ admin costs	Salaries, National Insurance, pension fund for training management and support staff	
	Salaries (etc) of direct trainers when not occupied in development or delivery of training	
	Recruitment and selection costs	
	Professional association and journal subscriptions	
	SUB-TOTAL	
Training of trainers	Fees for external courses, distance learning	
	Costs of internal courses	
	Salaries (etc) whilst being trained	
	SUB-TOTAL	
Delivery of training	Salaries (etc) whilst engaged in training	
	Trainers' travel and accommodation	
	Fees for external consultants, guest speakers, external courses, licensed use of copyright materials	
	Trainees' travel and accommodation	
	SUB-TOTAL	
Training development costs	Salaries (etc) of training staff whilst identifying training needs, developing training activities, evaluating effects of training	
	Fees to external consultants for similar services	
	Costs of visual aids, print, computer time, video production, etc	
	SUB-TOTAL	
	OVERALL TOTAL	

A second approach to judging whether or not training matters is to identify any instances where inadequate work performance is costing the organization money, and where suitable training might be expected to lead to improvements. The following checklist provides you with a framework for doing this.

ACTIVITY			
Checklist of examples of inadequate work performance which may respond to training			
Aspects of work performance	Does it happen here?	Best guess at £ cost	Best guess at £ gain by training
Customer complaints Equipment downtime Delivery delays Breakages Lost sales Accidents Quality failures Staff turnover Recruitment errors Ineffective training Uncontrolled overheads Bad debts Stock control problems Excessive inventory held Capacity under-utilized Contract deadlines missed Loss of market share Absenteeism Shortage of promotable staff Excessive overtime working *Add your own examples*			

A more subtle training cost to monitor is that incurred by poorly designed, badly focused training. This is the cost of learning irrelevant or incorrect things, and of incomplete learning. Whether or not this is a problem in your organization may – at present – be a matter of intuitive judgements rather than clear evidence but the techniques described in Chapter 6 will help you gather firm data on such questions of training quality.

A working definition of good training is that it is an investment (of organizational resources and individual effort) that yields identifiable improvements in job performance. The answer to the question, 'Does training matter?' is 'Yes, provided it is good training'. The notion of good training as the means to achieve improved job performance provides the essential linkage between corporate strategy and training strategy that is explored in the next section.

Corporate Strategy and Training Strategy

'Training strategy' is concerned with getting the right things done. 'Training validation' (broadly speaking) addresses the question of whether or not training has achieved what was intended. 'Training evaluation' focuses upon judgements about whether the training has been worthwhile. Validation and evaluation are discussed in Chapter 6, but need a preliminary mention here because they are inseparable from questions of training strategy.

Central to the concept of strategy is the idea of purpose. It is the contribution that training makes to the achievement of an organization's purposes that provides the justification for investment of resources of time, people and money in that training. It can be helpful to look at organizational purposes in terms of a four-category framework developed by Cameron[1]. All organizations, except universities, fit into this framework. The four categories are:

1. *Goal-directed organizations* which pursue specific targets (turnover, profit, market-share and the like); these measure their effectiveness by comparing actual against targeted performance.
2. *Resource-acquiring organizations* which measure success by their ability to replenish key input resources; for example, mineral resources for an extractive company, skilled programmers for a software house, or investment funds for a unit trust.
3. Organizations which judge their effectiveness in terms of their *internal functioning* – using such criteria as internal communications,

staff participation in decision-making, maintaining a 'quality' culture, or the level of internal conflict.

4. *Constituent-satisfying organizations* which exist principally to meet the needs of a particular group (or groups) of people; for example, advice bureaux, workers' cooperatives, governmental organizations. Commercial organizations, too, may be responsive to their particular constituents – shareholders, consumer groups, employees.

Cameron suggests that each organization is shaped by one of these purposes which is dominant, but that secondary purposes may also be significant. In terms of defining an organization's training strategy, it is essential to pinpoint which purposes actually dominate in a given situation. Note, in particular, that sometimes the formally stated corporate purposes may receive only lip-service; actual performance is shaped by the informal culture. Note too that it is quite usual to find different perceptions of the dominant organizational purpose at different levels in the hierarchy. Senior management commonly focus on a goal-directed view of effectiveness, whereas at supervisory level internal functioning – in the form of smoothly working teams, or cooperation between sections – often is the significant measure of effectiveness.

The link between corporate strategy and training is not trivial and should not be obscured. Trainers – whether 'formal' or 'informal' – need to know where the organization is going if they are to provide cost-effective training. Corporate strategic purpose is the bedrock on which rests something as apparently remote as a single learning objective within a particular training event. When organizational purposes and training objectives are in harmony, training is a powerful contributor to organizational success. When the connection is lacking, training becomes a luxurious overhead which can reasonably be presumed unnecessary.

However, defined corporate purposes – typically in the form of 'mission statements' – only start to make a difference to work performance when they have been translated into detailed task requirements for each individual. Otherwise, the cynical view that mission statements resemble obituaries rather than manifestos is likely to be correct. The problems come from two directions: bland generalities that change nothing and motivate no one; and obsolescence. In a fast-changing environment the definition of corporate purpose must be responsive.

Blandness is avoided by a structured cascading of mission goals into workplace practices and performance standards, at all levels. This alone goes a long way towards ensuring the relevance of training activities. Protection against obsolescence requires that corporate purpose is tested regularly against external reality, that the market drives the mission statement.

You may like to apply your understanding of your own organization's corporate strategy to the way you do your own job, using the activity which follows. With this and the other activities, you may like to write out your answers on a separate sheet of paper.

ACTIVITY
Training and organizational purposes

What is the dominant measure of effectiveness in this organization (in terms of Cameron's four categories)?

What (if any) differences can I identify between measures of effectiveness operating at different levels (or in different parts) of this organization?

What implications does this have for training in general in this organization?

What does this organization's mission statement (or equivalent) mean when I apply it to my own job? Do I do different things; do I do things in a different way; do I work to specific performance measures that relate to corporate purposes?

Do any of my answers suggest possible training needs for myself?

What actions can I usefully take to follow up this analysis?

What is a Training Need?

– Someone is not doing a job as well as they are capable of doing, because they are suffering from some shortfall in their knowledge or their skills. This can be conveniently given the shorthand description of an *improvement (or remedial) need* to do things better,

or

– Someone needs to acquire additional knowledge or skills in order to perform new or amended work tasks *in the near future*. This is an *anticipatory (or developmental)* need.

I have emphasized 'in the near future' because one of the least cost-effective uses of training is to provide anticipatory training too far in advance of the opportunity to use it. If people do not use what they have learned in training quite soon after that training is completed, then their learning suffers from what psychologists call 'decay of learning' and the rest of us call 'forgetting'.

The essence of a training need, then, is a gap between what exists and what is needed for optimum performance. When a piece of training is designed in response to such a need, several positive results follow:

- training content relates to job realities rather than to abstract principles;
- people undergoing training are much more likely to see the activity as useful and relevant – and therefore learn more readily;
- on-the-job performance improves;
- measurement of improved performance becomes more feasible.

Unfortunately, the ambitions for change in an organization are not always matched by appropriate means. In a variant of Parkinson's Law on expenditure decisions, it sometimes seems that the more grandiose the objectives for change, the more superficial the methods adopted. Policymakers may expect radical change in patterns of behaviour developed over decades, and expect it from brief, under-researched, and unreinforced 'quasi-training' events. Trainers (especially external suppliers) may collude with these unrealistic expectations, for the very human reason that there is a lot of money to be made. 'Snake-oil training' and 'blessing the crowds with a hosepipe' are two popular judgements from those on the receiving end. In Chapter 3, the methods for achieving well-designed training will be outlined and Chapter 5 gives further advice on getting value for money when employing external training resources.

What is not a Training Need?

The quick answer is: 'Anything that is neither an improvement need nor an anticipatory need'. However, there are a number of apparent needs that it is worth being on guard against because they lead to training that is neither effective nor value for money. In every case, the best insurance you can take is to ensure that a proper diagnostic analysis has been made before resources are committed to what may be inappropriate solutions.

1. *Rest and recreation*: There is nothing wrong with training being both interesting and enjoyable (it usually helps learning) but sometimes the means overtake the ends and training comes to be seen as a perk or a

status symbol ('All managers at my level go on the Senior Manager Programme'). Danger signs are when training events are evaluated primarily in terms of the quality of the hotel facilities or the acquisition of institutional ties and plaques.

2. *Country Club training:* This is a version of R&R training which is typified by comments such as 'It won't do any harm', which carry an implicit message that 'It probably will not make much difference either'. It is usually found where managers have little interest in or understanding of training; they may see their role as limited to making formal nominations of their staff onto available courses. Low expectations are usually matched by poor quality of provision, since no one cares whether the training works or not.

3. *Solutions in search of a problem:* This can be a problem both with internal trainers (who become over-attached to their favourite programmes) and, even more, with external suppliers who want you to buy what they have to sell (which, just sometimes, may meet your needs satisfactorily). Effective training must start from a diagnosis of the needs of your particular, unique situation; only then can appropriate solutions be developed (or, sometimes, be bought in, provided your needs are sufficiently general in nature).

4. *Badge engineering:* This is a variant of number 2 which typically involves putting your corporate logo on the front cover and an inserted message from the chief executive in the front of an otherwise standard package of material. 'Tailored' programmes can only justify that description if they are based on substantial in-house analysis of training needs and the finished product contains a substantial proportion of material that is specific to the commissioning organization.

5. *Fads:* Fads occur in training content and in training technology. It's usually worth questioning the invisibility of the Emperor's new clothes. No training technique is inherently 'best' – different methods work more effectively for different kinds of learning need. No method is any better than the diagnostic work that underpins it – 'rubbish in, rubbish out' applies just as much to training as to computer programming!

6. *Training as part of the employment package:* This can be an attractive inducement to potential recruits and there is nothing wrong with it in principle; where it may go wrong is in the execution. If training is provided *primarily* because it is part of the employment package, its purposes tend to be distorted. This is especially prone to happen if there is a corporate philosophy of 'we believe in personal development'. The consequence can be training for training's sake, without regard to organizational priorities.

7. *Solutionism*: When training needs are being investigated, some people will respond with statements that describe what they think the training solution ought to be, rather than what the underlying problem is. A typical statement would be, 'Smith needs communications training', which yields no guidance on what skill deficiency Smith is suffering from. Is it a problem when talking face-to-face, or on the telephone; is it letter writing skills, compiling reports, working in teams, or what? Effective diagnosis gets behind the label, the course name, to discover what is going wrong on the job.

The activity which follows invites you to question what training needs are being addressed by some current training activity with which you are acquainted.

ACTIVITY
Analysing the justification for a current training activity

1. Make a note of the training activity to be reviewed.

2. What need(s) does this training meet (what would you expect to see people doing differently after the training):
(a) for improved work performance?

(b) for anticipatory knowledge/skills?

3. Who asked for this training?

4. What justifications were originally offered?

5. What identifiable and/or measurable benefits were expected?

6. What can the person(s) who asked for the training now tell you about any differences it has made to the way they do their jobs?

7. What did the training cost to develop initially and then to run?

8. Do you feel that it represents value for money? Make a note of your reasons for that opinion.

9. What actions can I usefully take to follow up this analysis?

Motivation, Personality and Training

Training is not a form of psychotherapy. If managers are unhappy about the personalities of the people they manage, the problem usually lies either with the manager's own personality, with the recruitment process or with the reward system. Training can increase knowledge and enhance skills, within the capabilities of the trainees. Competent trainers will achieve better results than non-competent trainers.

However, if an organization can recruit only people with limited experience, low educational attainment, and poorly developed learning skills, then it must recognize that training can only do so much to raise the levels of employee competence. Restructuring ('de-skilling') jobs is likely to be a more fruitful solution in the short-to-medium term.

It is very common for confusion to arise between trainable skills and non-trainable personality traits, such as 'having a positive attitude' or being 'well-motivated'. These are useful attributes of personality, but whether or not they are demonstrated within work will depend on the management climate, the satisfactions (or their absence) in work tasks, the ways in which work performance is assessed and rewarded, the physical environment of work – but not on training. If an employee is 'well-motivated', training can provide the knowledge and skills through which that motivation will be demonstrated, but, with one important exception, if motivation is lacking then training will not provide it.

The exception arises where 'lack of motivation' is caused mainly by a fear of being seen to be ignorant or incompetent – in short, by a lack of training. A self-reinforcing positive spiral can be created by appropriate training, as illustrated in Figure 1.1.

Conclusion

This chapter has discussed the purposes of training in organizations and asked, 'Is training worth the investment?'. The nature of training needs has been summarized as 'needs for improvement' and 'anticipatory needs', either of which necessitate activities that will enhance knowledge and/or skills. The differences between skill acquisition, motivation and personality have been emphasized.

The common threads running through the discussion of strategy, training and evaluation are the importance of clear purposes (which provide both targets and criteria of achievement), of identifying results, and of assessing value.

A strategic focus ensures that the design and delivery of training

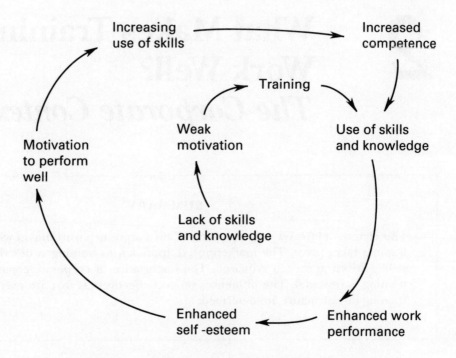

Figure 1.1 *The training/competence/motivation spiral*

activities matches real needs. Evaluation focuses upon judgements about the correctness of that strategy (including the means adopted) and particularly upon the outcomes that the strategy delivers. Efficient training design is grounded in a market-driven diagnostic process that responds to strategic concerns and forms the subject of the next chapter.

Note

1. Cameron K. (1980) 'Critical questions in assessing organizational effectiveness', in *Organizational Dynamics*, autumn, pp 66–80.

2 What Makes Training Work Well? *The Corporate Context*

▷   SUMMARY   ◁

This chapter addresses various aspects of the corporate environment within which training takes place. The marketing-led approach to training is described and a selling-driven approach criticized. The importance of corporate commitment to training is reviewed. The influences on cost-effectiveness that are exerted by the training infrastructure are described.

The Marketing-led Approach to Training

The marketing-led approach to training mirrors the principles of marketing that apply to products and services. It starts from an analysis of what the 'consumer' wants and needs. Training-needs analysis is the equivalent of the market research applied to consumer products. The consumer may be the manager who authorizes training for subordinates; or an individual participant in training activities; or the organization as a whole represented by, for example, the MD, the Director of Personnel or some form of joint management-employee board. The key question that managers should be hearing from trainers is, 'How can I best help you to achieve what you are employed to do?'.

A benefit of the marketing-led approach in training is that the customers can feel ownership of the proposed solutions to their problems. This is because the training solution takes account of their problem-diagnosing contribution and also of their responsibility for ensuring that the solution sticks. It then becomes more realistic for managers to think of training as an investment in their staff rather than a tax on their resources.

The three rules that follow all reflect a marketing-led approach to training in organizations.

PRACTICAL TIPS

Rule 3: Training should be treated as an investment which yields identifiable payoffs, rather than as an overhead which reduces profits.

Rule 4: Effective training leads to better job performance – that is its justification and any other benefit from training is secondary to that.

Rule 5: (The Golden Rule): Do not train unless you need to.

Marketing-led vs Selling-driven Approach to Training

The marketing-led approach needs to be distinguished from a selling-driven approach to training. In a 'selling' mode, training providers offer a fixed menu of training activities – typically presented in an annual courses brochure – to line management customers. There is an implicit (but often unjustified) assumption in the selling mode that these ready-made training events are in some way the fulfilment of the customer's requirements. It is the training equivalent of Henry Ford's 'You can have it in any colour, so long as it's black', and an ominous phrase to listen for is the trainer who says, 'This is the programme that we, the professionals in this area, have developed for you – we would suggest that you need this one or that one … '.

Training and personnel people often put a lot of energy into persuading people to attend these courses. A warning sign is the telephone call that says, 'We need to fill up several places on this course'. As frequently happens with pressurized sales, there is then a spate of last-minute cancellations. Course delegates are often in the dark about the reasons for their attendance (attributing it to the short-straw principle, to being most easily spared on the day, or just to bad luck). End-of-course 'happy-sheet' ratings are not matched by improvements in job performance. Over time, people become very resistant to attending such courses. The funding of training quite rightly comes into question and the more enterprising departments start to buy in training suppliers who are more responsive to what they need.

A common consequence of inadequate needs analysis (ie, poor market research) is a rash of last-minute withdrawals from courses; people attending training part-time ('I'm just popping out to check my desk'), or a half-hearted, tourist attitude of, 'I'm only here to see if this is of interest for other people'. What all these have in common is a lack of commitment from trainees mostly because the relevance of the training is in doubt, and typically because the diagnostic stage of training design is weak.

In contrast, the marketing-led approach starts from a very different position: an analysis of what the customer wants. It is underpinned by specific needs, and as Chapter 1 has already stated, there are only two ways in which training needs arise:

1. an improvement (or remedial) need to do things better;
2. an anticipatory (or development) need to do new things.

The essence of the marketing-led approach in training is to identify the gap between what exists and what is wanted. Training designed on that basis has strengths lacking in sales-driven training:

- the content of the training relates to work realities rather than to theory and abstract principles;
- people taking part in training are much more likely to see the activity as useful and relevant – and consequently learn better;
- the training is more likely to pay off through improved work performance;
- measurement of what the training has achieved becomes more feasible.

The short quiz that follows gives you a chance to review the extent to which training in your organization is either marketing-led or selling-driven. Reflect on how you (and perhaps your colleagues) feel about training in your organization. Tick a 'yes' or 'no' for each item.

ACTIVITY *Is training in your organization marketing-oriented?*	Yes	No
1. Training is seen as a perk for good behaviour		
2. Everybody has to complete a quota of so many days of training each year		
3. The training department sometimes has to ring around to fill vacant places on courses it runs		
4. If a course looks interesting in the brochures, someone is sent along to find out what it is like		
5. The biggest benefit from training is the opportunity to meet people from other parts of the organization		
6. To qualify for incentive bonuses, sales people must have attended at least one training course in the year		
7. When budgets are tight, it is common sense to cut training expenditure first		
8. We believe in the importance of training		
9. If managers are not sent to business school by a certain age, it indicates that they will not be promoted to senior posts		
Total		

Comments on the quiz

1. Training is seen as a perk for good behaviour: this suggests that the organization has lost sight of the connection between work performance and training provision.
2. Everybody has to complete a quota of so many days of training each year: again, this is the kind of goal-displacement that distorts provision of cost-effective training. It is good to have a culture that encourages training as a worthwhile part of worklife; but different people have differing training needs which uniform quotas will match only by chance.
3. The training department sometimes has to ring around to fill vacant places on courses it runs: this immediately raises the questions, 'Why is

there so little support for this course?', 'Who asked for it in the first place?', 'Why is it being sold to you?'.

4. If a course looks interesting in the brochures, someone is sent along to find out what it is like: it is understandable that you want to find out more about a training activity before committing numbers of people to it. However, people attending as 'tourists' are prone to have low involvement in the training which may distort the feedback you get. More fundamentally, a training activity should not have got to the stage of being run, without managers being involved in the diagnosis of needs and agreement of the content.

5. The biggest benefit from training is the opportunity to meet people from other parts of the organization: so set up interdepartmental working parties, social events, sporting functions ... meeting people is a legitimate benefit from training, but it certainly should not be seen as the biggest benefit!

6. To qualify for incentive bonuses, sales people must have attended at least one training course in the year: see number 2.

7. When budgets are tight, it is common sense to cut training expenditure first: it is certainly one of the *easiest* things to cut, but by no means the most cost-effective. The short-term saving is usually more than offset by the medium-term deterioration in levels of competence (assuming, of course, that the training was responding to its market in the first place).

8. We believe in the importance of training: this is fine as a statement of commitment, but a trap if you really want to have training that pays for itself. Belief in training implies a lack of evidence that it affects work performance. That in turn suggests the training has a weak diagnostic foundation and is not market-led.

9. If managers are not sent to business school by a certain age, it indicates that they will not be promoted to senior posts: the risks are two-fold. First, this may reflect a self-fulfilling prophecy whereby only those managers who have attended that course get senior promotions. Second, it may become little more than a 'club' symbol for those who have passed that career hurdle. In neither case is there any reason to *assume* a close connection between the training and the remedial or development needs of the individual.

In summary, every tick in the 'yes' column is a warning sign that training may be driven by a need to sell courses rather than led by a marketing analysis of the needs of the potential customers for the training.

Corporate Commitment to Training

Managers themselves need to know where the organization is heading before they can sensibly contribute to training, so one starting point for effective, market-led training lies with clearly stated and widely communicated corporate purposes.

Another, equally important issue, is the example that each level in the organizational structure sets to the next level. Lip-service to training is not uncommon amongst senior managers but the implicit message of lip-service is 'Do as I say, not as I do'. If, however, senior managers do play an active role in the development of, say, middle managers, the latter are more likely to follow that example and contribute to the training of their supervisory staff, and so on down the line.

By 'an active role' I mean that managers involve themselves in such activities as coaching individuals, taking part in workshops, making authoritative inputs to courses, and the like. It is not an active role to make a brief appearance to open or close a course nor to go along to the closing dinner 'to find out what it has been like for participants'. The corollary of this is that managers must be prepared for such a role. There can be few things more damaging to an individual's credibility than to be required to perform a task for which he or she is untrained. To enable managers to contribute to training, they need some of the knowledge and skills of the professional trainer and this need is addressed in Chapter 5.

It is always as well to remember that managers mainly do the things that they get rewarded for doing. It is therefore important that any appraisal of performance and any change of salary or bonus are based in part upon what a manager has been doing to progress the training of the people who work for him or her. If the organizational culture expects that managers will run around like headless chickens, engaged in continual fire-fighting, then it is easy to predict that neither forward planning nor cost-effective training are likely to be found there.

PRACTICAL TIPS

Rule 6: Set a good example at all levels in the organization.
Rule 7: Reward managers who play an active and constructive role in training.
Rule 8: Ensure that managers have the skills they need in order to contribute to effective training.

The review document opposite is addressed to managers. It provides a structure for you to review some very fundamental questions about the state of training provision in your organization. There are no right answers; what you do with your answers really depends upon whether you are content that things are 'good enough' or you feel the need for improvements. If the latter, then this book provides a comprehensive range of measures that will increase the cost-effectiveness of training.

The Training Infrastructure

The physical context within which training takes place is another factor determining cost-effectiveness. The training infrastructure affects results at two levels. First, inadequate facilities make it difficult to deliver effective training: you need a quiet, reasonably comfortable room equipped with chairs and tables that can be easily rearranged as the activity dictates. An overhead projector and flipchart are the minimum equipment needed.

At a second level, training facilities affect learning through the subliminal messages that they convey to trainees. Where the facilities are basic to the point of discomfort or distraction the message is clear: training does not matter and the organization does not really want to have to provide it. At the other extreme, where facilities are luxurious and/or the location exotic, the underlying message is only slightly different: training does not matter, because the trainees are where they are because of their status or as a reward for good behaviour. It is probably only called 'training' for taxation purposes.

Between the broom cupboard next to the 20-ton press and the country club facility with its own golf course, there is plenty of scope to provide training facilities that do offer effectiveness, do not cost a fortune, and convey the message: 'We take training seriously and expect it to pay-off through improved performance'.

Conclusion

This chapter has been concerned with the question, 'What makes training work well?', with the focus upon aspects of the corporate environment within which training takes place. The marketing-led approach to training has been contrasted with the less cost-effective selling-driven approach. The importance of corporate commitment to training has been reviewed and the influence of the training infrastructure on cost-

ACTIVITY

Corporate commitment to training

1. Is there any internal document that links training provision to corporate strategy? Does the Annual Report include any statement about investment in training and development?

2. How frequently is the training strategy (if any) reviewed?

3. What (if any) part do senior managers play in training?

4. What training (if any) do senior managers undertake to maintain or improve their own knowledge and skills? How are the pay-offs from this assessed?

5. What does a senior manager do to ensure appropriate training for the middle managers who report to him or her?

6. What do senior managers do to ensure that middle-level managers make appropriate training provision for their subordinates?

7. Do managers at any level actively collaborate with trainers (eg, to reinforce learning through pre- and post-training briefings; to contribute to training activities)?

8. Is your perception of your organization's trainers that they are providers of courses, or that they are a problem-solving resource and catalyst of productive change in the organization?

9. What do you think of the service you as a manager get from the organization's trainers?

10. Is a period of secondment in training regarded as a positive career move, or as an alternative to involuntary redundancy?

11. How is the training budget determined?

12. What kinds of justification are given for training expenditure?

13. When your business is under pressure in the market, is the training budget cut or increased?

14. What measures of cost-effectiveness are applied either to in-house training or to training that is bought in from external suppliers? Are these measures satisfactory for their purpose? In what form (if any) is this information communicated to senior managers?

effectiveness described. Methods to develop a collaborative working partnership between managers and trainers – certainly one aspect of the corporate environment – merits separate treatment and is discussed in depth in Chapter 4.

Chapter 3 addresses the question, 'What Makes Training Work Well?' from the perspective of good training design.

3   What Makes Training Work Well?
Design Issues

▷   SUMMARY   ◁

This chapter reviews the factors that make for effective training. It provides a comprehensive overview of the training cycle: diagnostics, design, delivery and evaluation, including the issue of matching training to the individual.

Introduction

As a manager you may begin to feel that this chapter has a strongly technical flavour which, perhaps, would make it more appropriate reading for the full-time trainer. May I ask you to put your reservations 'on hold'; this book is about cost-effective training and the 'effective' part of that equation does call for a good understanding of what makes the difference between flashy but ineffectual training and training that makes a measurable difference to work performance.

There are two directions in which you can apply the content of this chapter. The first is to use its guidelines when you yourself are preparing training, however informal, for your own staff. The guidelines will apply when you include a training element within, say, a monthly meeting; or, as a sales manager, review a visit to a customer with your sales person, as you drive to the next appointment; or when you make a set-piece speech to a company conference. These are all instances where the rules for cost-effective training can be applied, to the benefit of your own credibility and the organization's effectiveness.

The second opportunity to apply the content of this chapter arises when you are commissioning internal training or buying places on external courses. You can use the guidelines as a yardstick by which you can assess the quality of whatever you are being offered.

The Training Cycle

There is a view of training design and delivery that reduces the whole process to two stages:

1. read up on the subject, and
2. tell the trainees all about it (possibly also giving them some opportunity for practice).

This model has the virtue of simplicity but not, unfortunately, of effectiveness. The latter is more likely to result from a model that is both more complicated and more realistic – the model of training as a cyclical process, illustrated in Figures 3.1 and 3.2.

In Figure 3.1 the elements of diagnosing the learning need, designing and then delivering the training, and providing follow-up reinforcement have been broken down into a number of discrete stages. As it stands, however, the model is linear rather than cyclical. The training has been put together in a more effective way, but there is no way of knowing whether or not the training itself is having any effect. The loop is closed by the feedback element of 'evaluation' – the range of techniques (discussed in more depth in Chapter 6) that asks three important questions:

- has this training done what was intended?
- was what was achieved worth the effort?
- is there a better way of doing it?

Figure 3.2 shows the loop completed by the element of evaluation. In an ideal world, evaluation would not be necessary because all training would be perfectly designed, skilfully implemented and thoroughly reinforced in the workplace. Even in the real world, much can be done to minimize the need for evaluation, through properly considered training design. This chapter covers the fundamentals of effective design, drawing upon the author's experiences during 15 years of evaluation research and consultancy.

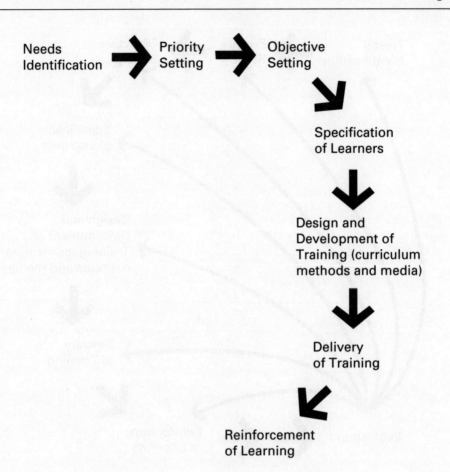

Figure 3.1 *The training cycle (linear version)*

PRACTICAL TIP

Rule 9: Cutting corners around the training cycle doesn't yield cheaper training; it yields ineffective training whatever the cost.

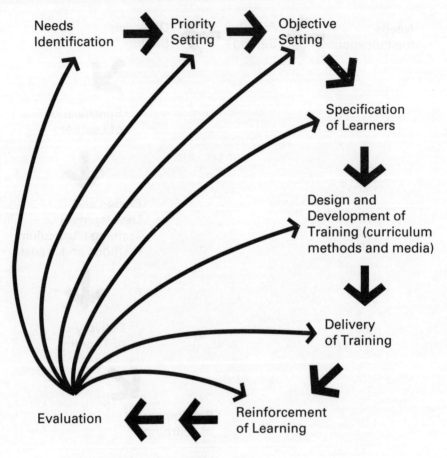

Figure 3.2 *The training cycle (with evaluation feedback)*

Diagnostics

You cannot have cost-effective training without accurate diagnosis of needs, which means going out into the workplace to discover just what it is that people need to learn in order to become more effective in their jobs. Diagnosis starts from such questions as, 'What are people doing (or not doing) that needs to be changed?', or, 'What would you, the manager, like to *see* people doing differently after they have been trained?'. The emphasis must be on the *observed* behaviour that needs to be changed, or introduced. It is never a diagnostic response to say, 'What this person needs is a course on...', or, 'This person has a bad attitude to...'.

'Smith finds it hard to ask qualifying questions when with sales prospects' is a much more useful diagnostic statement, on which practical training measures can be based, than any of the following statements:

'Smith should be a more outgoing person',

'Smith lacks motivation and enthusiasm', or

'Smith needs a sales refresher course.'

This emphasis on observable work behaviour sidesteps the trap of stating training needs in terms of the attitudes or personality traits of an idealized occupant of the job. Personality change is difficult to achieve, takes a long time and lies within the remit of therapists rather than trainers. 'Personality' as an element of individual performance is something that should be sorted out at the recruitment stage, or subsequently by counselling.

The focus upon observable behaviour also helps to avoid 'awareness' being presented as a training goal. 'Awareness' is *the* weasel word in selling-driven training. It should immediately put any buyer of training services on guard. It indicates training in the 'nice-to-know' rather than 'need-to-know' category; it indicates too that no practical benefits are to be expected; above all it warns that there has been no adequate diagnosis of learning needs. 'Awareness' events are what you get when neither trainer nor management client knows clearly what they want to be done differently at work. Conversely, given proper diagnostic data, training can develop relevant knowledge and skills, rather than a vague awareness.

One of the best pay-offs from diagnostic analysis comes in the form of management involvement in training. Managers are able to feel a sense of ownership of the training events that result. Following on from this, they are more likely to play a reinforcing role pre- and post-training. Trainers themselves benefit from better quality of information on which to base their training designs.

A second major benefit from proper needs analysis is that post-training evaluation of cost-effectiveness is made easier. The connection between diagnostics and evaluation works through the detailed training objectives that should be prepared for every training event. The process works in in the following manner.

The initial diagnosis of needs is translated into a set of detailed learning objectives which specify everything that trainees need to learn. Properly defined objectives should contain a criterion by which the trainer or manager can assess the extent to which the objectives have been met. It is a useful test of how well a training objective has been drawn to ask, 'How can I tell when this objective has been achieved?'. When objectives are set and evaluation criteria defined in parallel, this proves much more economical of trainers' time compared to the laborious task of adding evaluation measures retrospectively to an existing training design.

The diagnosis of developmental or anticipatory needs poses one special concern: how far ahead should a training need be anticipated? Sometimes, people are offered training for a job to which they have prospects of promotion. It can be a fine balance between providing skills in readiness for that future job and providing them too early so that much may have been forgotten by the time that they are needed. Retention of knowledge and skills depends mainly on having opportunities to use them.

Lastly, a diagnostic foundation for training design guards against a number of common but spurious justifications of training (described in Chapter 1 under the heading 'What is not a training need?').

PRACTICAL TIPS

Rule 10: A meaningful training need is one that describes required changes in work behaviour – *not* attitudes, personality, or awareness needs.

Rule 11: The value of the diagnostic process is much enhanced when it is made a joint collaboration between trainers (who know how to use a range of diagnostic techniques) and managers (who know where the problems and pressure points are).

Rule 12: It is a considerable economy of effort – and contributes to much sharper training objectives – to develop training objectives and evaluation measures in parallel rather than separately.

The two activities that follow provide you with the opportunity to review the diagnostic basis of the training with which you are familiar (or the lack of such a basis). The first activity invites you to focus upon one specific piece of training of which you have some knowledge or experience; the second takes a broader perspective by asking what kinds of diagnostic activity take place in your organization.

ACTIVITY

Reviewing the diagnostic foundation of existing training

1. Name of training activity to be reviewed:

2. What justification was originally presented for this training?

3. What current or anticipated work need(s) does the training meet?

4. What changes in work behaviour or performance standards would you expect to observe after the training?

5. What, if any, evidence is there that the training has in fact made a difference to job performance?

6. In your judgement, are the identified changes in performance such that they justify the time and money invested in the training?

7. In the light of your answers to these questions, what changes would you like to see put in place?

ACTIVITY

Does your organization adopt a diagnostic approach to identifying training needs?

1. Who (if anybody) conducts reviews of training needs:
   - regularly:
   - occasionally:

2. List any of the following training diagnostic techniques that are used in your organization:*
   - Performance appraisal
   - Critical incident diary
   - Behaviour observation
   - Job analysis
   - Analysis of performance data
   - Interview
   - Questionnaire
   - Waiting for fires to fight

3. Do you think that any of these methods is over-used or used in the wrong contexts? Where might it be useful to introduce other methods for diagnosing training needs?

4. In the light of your answers to these questions, what changes would you like to see put in place?

---

*As this book is written primarily for managers, who I would not expect to conduct the diagnostic work themselves, I have not provided what would need to be a fairly extended description of these techniques. If you need more information, then your organization's own trainers should be able to help.

Diagnostics and Appraisal Systems

Appraisal can be the opportunity for a constructive dialogue between manager and subordinate which can spotlight training and development needs. Appraisal subsequent to training can be an opportunity to evaluate the benefits from that activity.

The limitations of appraisal are two-fold: first, it may occur only once a year or even every other year. Discussion of training needs may be stored up for an annual binge, creating an excessive lead time between a need arising, being identified at appraisal and finally training being provided.

Second, the annual appraisal may fall prey to 'menu-bashing', when it is seen as an occasion to browse through course brochures to pick out those events which have not yet been attended, rather than to identify performance deficiencies to which training solutions may then be sought.

Determining Priorities

Once the diagnostic information has been collected, priorities for action need to be decided. First, though, non-training alternatives should be considered. Training may not be the right solution, or it may not be the most cost-effective solution. There may be several options that need to be weighed: eg, redesign of the job (possibly de-skilling); recruitment of people with the required competence; clarification of the diagnosis (perhaps a training need in subordinate staff may actually reflect a performance deficiency in the supervisor or manager); and of course training itself. Sometimes an organizational problem is labelled as 'training' when it is actually a management hot potato which nobody wants to end up holding.

Once it is decided which needs really represent training issues, priorities must usually be set. Training budgets are rarely open-ended! The choice of priorities should reflect the anticipated benefits, in relation to corporate strategy. However, in practice, the most usual influences on priority-setting are:

- the money available;
- legal requirements (eg, for safety training);
- organizational politics (who shouts loudest, gets most);
- trainer preferences (running the courses they most enjoy);
- the prestige attaching to the proposed 'solution'
  and lastly – and unfortunately often least in influence –
- organisational strategy.

Effectiveness can often be improved simply by making the basis of prioritizing explicit. Given cooperation between trainers and managers, with training regarded as an integral part of corporate effectiveness, the allocation of resources between competing training projects can be treated much more like any other investment decision.

Setting Learning Objectives

It is not enough to identify learning needs and then to move directly to assembling the content of a training event. First, detailed learning objectives must be specified for each part of the training. These are essential:

- to ensure that all necessary knowledge and skill elements are represented, and
- to provide the benchmarks that enable subsequent measurement of how effective that training has been.

Learning objectives should state in behavioural terms precisely what a person will be able to do differently as a result of training. Ineffective training tends to adopt a scattergun approach, rather than pinpointing the target. Ineffective training is characterized by learning objectives which use vague phrases such as:

'... will gain an awareness of ...', or
'... should understand ...', or, worst of all,
'...will develop a positive attitude towards...'.

I do not doubt that sometimes attitudes shape behaviour (although the reverse is also true), but at a practical level I find it a great energy-saver to work with those features of people which are accessible to observation. Trainers can directly influence behavioural skills; managers can see what their staff are doing at work and can reward good performance or correct bad. Second-guessing what is happening in people's heads may be fun but it isn't reliable.

Effective learning objectives state unambiguously what trained persons will be capable of doing back in their jobs. The quality of the objectives is the first thing that any buyer of training – whether it is in-house or an external course – should assess critically. Although actuality often falls short of the ideal, it is always worth looking for the three core elements of a properly drafted learning objective. These three elements are:

- *Desired behaviour:* this may take the form of physical action, interpersonal behaviour, verbal responses, or writing. It must be observable, not a matter for inference. 'Behaviour' excludes such phenomena as attitudes, motivation or personality traits.
- *Conditions for performance:* this is a statement of the limitations under which the behaviour must be demonstrated, eg, 'Will write answers to test questions whilst having access to a technical reference manual'.

- *Standard of performance*: this is the acceptable level at which the skill must be performed or knowledge demonstrated. Setting standards can be difficult and somewhat arbitrary especially in respect of interpersonal skills, but it is worth the effort to find reasonably consistent standards even here. It provides a focus both for the learning process and for measuring its effects.

You may like to try an audit of the quality of learning objectives for two or three training activities in your organization, using the activity document which follows. You may find it useful to audit training produced by different trainers or training of different kinds (eg, technical, managerial, interpersonal skills, sales, etc). You may also wish to share with colleagues the workload of such an audit.

ACTIVITY

Learning objectives quality audit

Select a current training activity and review its training objectives (or a sample of these).

1. The title of the training activity

2. List five sample objectives

3. Consider your judgements of the adequacy of these objectives, on the following criteria:

    - based upon an identified need?
    - explicit, precise wording?
    - specifies the behaviour, the conditions and the performance standard required?
    - can be readily checked by observation?

4. What do I wish to see changed?

5. How will these changes be brought about?

Specification of Learners

Well-designed training takes account of the trainees' previous knowledge, their work experience and their previous experience of the learning process itself. In some instances it may be necessary also to take account of literacy and language skills or learning difficulties. Where training may impact upon learners with physical or visual disabilities, care must be taken to ensure that they are not excluded from some activities by the way that the learning task has been set up. Effective training also takes account of learning-style preferences – the fact that different personalities learn best in different ways. As a general observation about all training, it is also important that training content is reviewed in order to eliminate sexist or racist references.

It is essential that training builds on trainees' existing foundation of knowledge and skills, without too great a gap for comprehension. This means that at the diagnostic stage information should be collected about the existing levels of ability amongst the target group.

Age is sometimes raised as an issue faced by trainers. However, whilst mental ability does peak between the ages of 18 and 25, the decline over the entire lifespan is normally no more than 5–10 per cent of capacity. At the same time this decline is likely to be offset by the older person's greater maturity and ability to use what is learned.

Older learners have often accumulated more experience and this forms part of their personal identity; they are likely to respond defensively if the value of their experience is challenged. As much as is appropriate, the learning process should try to increase their understanding of their experience. It must be recognized, though, that the experience which can constitute a valuable resource may also constitute a barrier to change; it is thus all the more important that older learners share in the initial diagnostic process. The training itself should have a problem-solving emphasis, offering learning that can be applied in a practical way. Note, too, that older learners are less willing to admit to mistakes and consequently persist with incorrectly learned behaviours unless the trainer identifies and corrects these quickly.

Design and Development

The selection of content, methods and media is the stage at which far too much training starts and finishes. Design of training without prior diagnostics, or subsequent evaluation of worth, is the commonest cause of ineffectiveness.

It is important to note that even when good diagnostic work has been carried out, there can be a a failure to translate specific learning needs into the training 'product'. What sometimes happens is that the content is not built up from the detailed foundation provided by the diagnosed knowledge and skill needs. Instead, it is drawn directly from books or borrowed from other training material that is concerned with that subject area in a more-or-less general way. The consequence can be that the content lacks relevance and immediacy to trainees. The actual workplace activities and problems of the trainees are overlooked. Identified needs must firstly be translated into clear learning objectives and only then into content.

The design and development stage deals with four elements:

1. The *methods* by which the subject matter is to be put across (eg, group discussion, role-play, etc). For example, a skill-training objective – whether a physical skill like operating a lathe, or an interpersonal skill like selling – is unlikely to be achieved through passive methods such as lecture or watching a film, however entertaining. Skill-acquisition demands demonstration and individual practice.

2. The subject matter, or *content*, to be conveyed to the learners. Content may include such material as a role-play briefing note; a detailed case study for analysis; a set of memos and documents for an in-tray exercise; or it may consist of instructions for a physical task such as machining a piece of metal. What matters is that the content is relevant and credible so that, say, health workers are not presented with case studies based on, say, supermarket retailing.

Content design is also concerned with the sequencing of materials and with planning for reinforcement of learning and correction of errors. Wherever possible, too, the design should take account of the preferred learning styles of course participants.[1]

3. The *media* employed in support of the training method (such as overhead projector slides, video or computer). Never treat an audio-visual aid as an end in itself. Film and video need to be integrated with exercises and structured discussions if their benefits are to be realized (see Appendix for an example of a video support checklist). Another common (and non-cost-effective) error is the 'chips with everything' syndrome typified by over-investment in a particular medium (such as computer-based learning or videodisc). The upfront system cost may be so great that the technique is used for every training activity, regardless of appropriateness.

4. The *structuring* of the training activity to achieve the best possible learning. The central concepts here are sequencing of learning, reinforcement (practice and feedback), and transfer.

Sequencing has three elements:
- the build-up of parts of a skill or task into the whole (in general, adults prefer to learn by what is called 'cumulative part-learning' in which each part is linked to what is known already);
- the need to move each training activity through a 'learning cycle' of experience, reflection, theory and practice (see Figure 3.3 adapted from Kolb *et al*[2]); and
- the need to take account of 'learning curves' which account for loss of attention, fatigue and decay of learning.

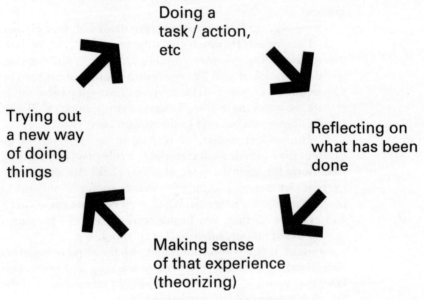

Doing a task / action, etc

Reflecting on what has been done

Making sense of that experience (theorizing)

Trying out a new way of doing things

Figure 3.3 *The learning cycle*

Learning activities should be broken up by rest breaks and changes of activity (the adult span of attention averages about 20 minutes). Learning peaks shortly after the end of a training session, when the brain has had the opportunity to absorb the new material. Thereafter, without reinforcement (through practice and from line managers) learning decays rapidly. As much as 80 per cent of a lecture will have been lost within 24 hours if there has been no reinforcement.[3] However, too much repetitive practice is counter-productive. Trainees should never end a practice session immediately after doing an action incorrectly: this is the action they are most likely to recall in the future. Feedback during practice should be provided immediately, whilst recollections are still fresh. It is more effective to encourage correct behaviours than to criticize those that are incorrect.

You can review the extent to which an existing piece of training has been satisfactorily structured by using the checklist on sequencing and reinforcement that follows.

ACTIVITY

Design structure quality audit

Select a current training activity and review its structure against the following checklist headings:

1. Sequencing of learning –
   - builds up logically, part-by-part;
   - uses cycle of doing/reflecting/understanding/trying out.

2. Learning curves –
   - short sessions with regular breaks and/or changes of activity;
   - fatigue plateaux avoided;
   - learning progress reviewed within each session.

3. Skill practice –
   - complex learning tasks broken into segments;
   - incorrect responses speedily corrected;
   - skills practised in realistic situations;
   - feedback given in a timely and constructive way.

4. Transfer of learning –
   - learning elements continually related to work applications;
   - training content relevant to trainees' jobs;
   - provision for manager's de-briefing and reinforcement post-training.

Delivery of Training

This is the stage at which training is most often judged 'good' or 'bad', on the strength of the trainer's performance skills (or those of a manager delivering training) in creating end-of-course euphoria. However, if you are concerned with effectiveness rather than entertainment, it is worth reflecting that undue emphasis on the presentation can overwhelm the content and minimize learning. Of course trainers must be able to hold the attention of their audiences – once the trainees are comatose, not even sleep-learning techniques will rescue the situation – but that requires thorough preparation rather than flash presentation.

When you are reviewing the effectiveness of delivery of training, there are broadly three groups of activity to watch for:

- presenting information and managing group activities, exercises, etc;
- generating interest and active participation amongst trainees;
- handling conflict in appropriate ways.

'Presentation skills' include planning, preparation of materials, public speaking, discussion-leading and use of audio-visual aids. These skills do matter: the first requirement for learning is that the audience continues to pay attention to the trainer.

Experienced trainers will often enrich their training by personalizing the presentation by *relevant* anecdotes. However, they should avoid stories that represent a put-down of other people and above all not get carried away with their 'war-stories' of how things used to be. Effective presentation requires rehearsal so that the training content is at the trainer's fingertips. Credibility is greatly enhanced when trainers run events without constant reference to notes or prompt cards.

Generating participation means that the trainer develops rapport with course members, using questions skilfully in the classroom. It means creation of training events that encourage active involvement rather than passive listening. The costs of low participation are failure to learn for trainees and damaged self-esteem for the trainer.

Trainers need to be able to respond constructively to conflict between themselves and trainees, or to conflicts amongst the latter. They may also wish on occasion to make conflict itself the focus of training.

Reinforcement of Learning

This important constituent of cost-effective training will be discussed both under the heading of 'Manager–trainer partnership' and within the context of design and development of training activities. Nothing further needs to be added here.

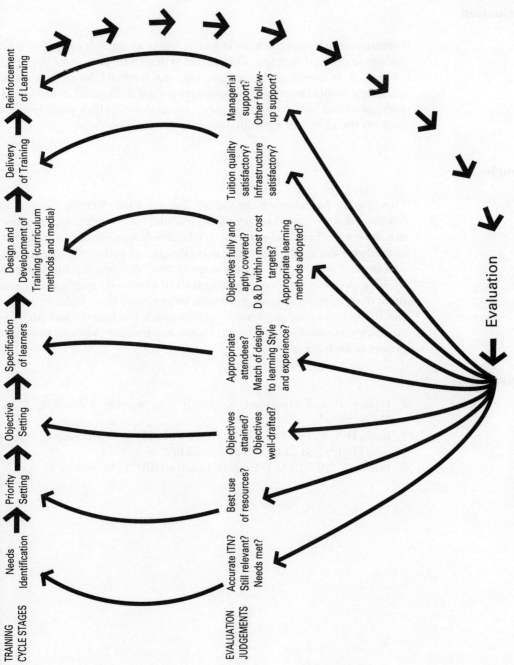

Figure 3.4 *The training cycle (including evaluation questions)*

Evaluation

Evaluation is perhaps the most important step, along with diagnostics, in the whole cycle of training. The subject is dealt with in greater depth in Chapter 6. It is evaluation that provides the feedback loops that make training a cyclical process. The loops are shown in Figure 3.4; each loop addresses particular evaluation questions, as shown, which provide feedback on the effectiveness of that stage in the training cycle.

Conclusion

This chapter has reviewed the factors that make for effective training. It has provided a detailed survey of the training cycle comprising diagnostics, design, delivery and evaluation. Effective design needs to use a range of methods and media but, while good design lies at the core of training, it is imperative that the design stage is not mistaken for the *whole* of training preparation. Accurate diagnosis of needs and systematic assessment of training effectiveness are even more essential: no training design can be stronger than the foundation on which it is based – and no cost-effectiveness equation can be struck for any training, without the techniques of evaluation.

Notes

1. Honey, P and Mumford, A (1986) *The Manual of Learning Styles*, Maidenhead.
2. Kolb, D A, Rubin, I M and McIntyre J M (1979) *Organizational Psychology*, Englewood Cliffs, NJ: Prentice-Hall.
3. Buzan, T (1974) *Use Your Head*, London: BBC Publications.

4 What Makes Training Work Well? *Managers and Trainers in Partnership*

▷   SUMMARY   ◁

In Part 1 of this chapter, methods to develop a collaborative working partnership between managers and trainers are presented. In Part 2, guidelines are given for buying in training services and employing consultants, in particular addressing the question: 'How do you ensure that you get what you ask for?'.

PART 1

Manager–Trainer Partnership: Can it Happen?

Now and then studies of training effectiveness throw up unexpected findings. One such result came from an evaluation that I undertook of training for technical and professional specialists in a large industrial company. This was the discovery that whether or not participants received an adequate briefing from their line managers was a better predictor of the use they made of the course content than was any other factor including the quality of the training itself.

Of course, pre-course briefing is not the only action managers can take to reinforce what the trainers are doing. However, it would be a mistake simply to think in terms of a number of distinct tasks that managers can do to supplement the things the trainers themselves do. Rather, it is necessary, when we address cost-effectiveness in training, to consider a philosophy or way of working that puts the emphasis upon partnership between trainers and managers at all stages of the training process.

57

Why should managers bother? They may well ask, 'Isn't training the job of trainers? Don't managers have enough to do already?'. Or they may feel that a very satisfactory job is already being done by the manager who says, 'I personally give my staff the instructions on how to get to the training centre, and I wish them luck as they leave'. Remarks such as these are not uncommon from managers who send their staff on training courses. Their involvement in the training process is limited, by and large, to signing the nomination form beforehand and approving the travelling expenses afterwards.

Note too that trainers sometimes go out of their way to discourage managers from taking too much interest in what they do. Trainers may put up 'no trespassing' signs around their domain and, falsely secure within the walls of the training centre, delude themselves that they 'know best' what their customers need. Trainers may write course brochures for trainers rather than for recipients of training. Often the course content is listed, but rarely the *benefits* that should be expected from the event. This not only discourages pre-training discussion between manager and participant, it also reinforces the impression that training is sealed off from real work life.

The main reason for making the effort comes back to the title of this book and, presumably, the reasons why you are reading it: to make training cost-effective. Managers despatch staff on training activities with little preparation and minimal expectation of benefits when – *if they knew what to do* – the manager could greatly increase the return from that person's investment of time and energy. Likewise, trainers can – *by collaboration with line managers* – do much to ensure that training addresses the right issues and that the way it is delivered encourages trainees to carry their new skills back to their jobs.

So what can be done to create a partnership to which both contribute? Figure 4.1 shows a framework for tackling these issues.

What Figure 4.1 emphasizes is just how important are management actions before and after training. The things that happen in the left-hand part (labelled 'Workplace Activities') are at least as critical as the training activities within the right-hand part.

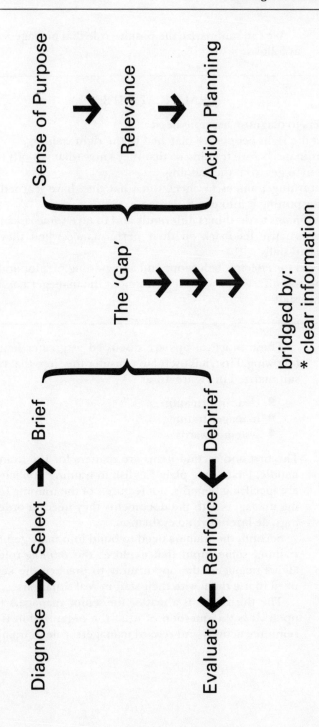

Training Activities (Mainly Trainers)

Sense of Purpose → Relevance → Action Planning

The 'Gap' → → →

bridged by:
* clear information
* manager training
* system rewards

Workplace Activities (Mainly Managers)

Diagnose → Select → Brief

Evaluate ← Reinforce ← Debrief

Figure 4.1 *Manager–trainer partnership: getting it right*

We can summarize the positive role that managers can play in training as follows:

PRACTICAL TIPS

1. Help trainers to diagnose learning needs.
2. Ensure that the right people are matched to the right training.
3. Brief subordinates before training so that they know what pay-offs their manager expects them to get from the training.
4. De-brief returning trainees to check out what they have learned and agree a timetable for putting it into practice.
5. Allow subordinates to do things differently and to take some risks.
6. Provide constructive feedback on their performance when they try out new knowledge and skills.
7. Act as a model for effective behaviour and as a guiding mentor and coach.
8. Evaluate the cost-effectiveness of the investment the manager has made in training his or her staff.

These practical tips are discussed at greater length in the sections following. First, it is useful to consider the steps that can make it happen, summarized in Figure 4.1 as:

- clear information
- manager training
- system rewards

The first and second items are matters for the training department to handle. First, using plain English in training publicity and other materials; specifying benefits, not features, of the training on offer; and providing managers with the documents they need in order to conduct briefings, de-briefings and evaluation.

Second, the trainers need to build into management and supervisory training some input that explores the *training* role of managers and allows managers the opportunity to practice the key skills before they need to use them with their staff in real situations.

The third item is a matter for senior managers to reflect (and act) upon. It is the question of what the organization is prepared to do to reinforce actively and reward managers' role in training.

Manager–Trainer Partnership: Putting it into Effect

Identifying training needs

Line managers are usually the people best placed to recognize performance deficiencies amongst employees within their area of responsibility. The detailed identification of needs and the setting of learning objectives will generally be the trainer's task, but the initial highlighting and prioritizing of current (or anticipated) problems is a key task for the manager. Note the essential difference between identifying performance or behaviour problems that may respond to a training solution and 'solutionism' (Chapter 1) where the training activity is itself put forward as if it were the training need. For example, to assert, 'What this person needs is a course in communications skills', is solutionism; by contrast, 'This person has difficulty in responding to telephone complaints from customers', is a useful diagnosis on which effective training can be built.

Selecting participants for training events

There are two broad methods for selection, either of which may be appropriate according to the circumstances. One is to select all people within a defined job category to undergo training, for example, to require that all new sales people attend a product knowledge presentation. The other method is to match the needs of the individual and the training, eg, 'Jones is poor at negotiating and this course will address those areas of weakness'.

What makes for ineffective selection is delegated attendance ('I should attend this time management course, but as I am too busy, you can go on my behalf'); attendance as last-minute substitute ('Smith is off sick – as we've paid for the course, you'd better go'); or the short-straw principle ('Personnel is pushing us to fill a place on this course – you're the only one I can spare at the moment').

It would be quite wrong to dump the blame for poor selection simply onto managers. More often than not, the problem of mismatched training arises simply because nobody has taken the trouble to show managers a better way of doing it. The difficulty may be that the manager just does not have a clear grasp of what is the purpose of the training, or that the skills of briefing and de-briefing have never been touched upon in management training.

Pre-training briefing and post-training de-briefing

The benefit is very clear: when trainees know what they are going to do and why the training is thought necessary, then they are primed to learn and to use what they acquire. The return on investment is also very high: a matter of perhaps 20 minutes for the pre-briefing and the same for de-briefing, set against the waste incurred by attending perhaps several days of training without getting the full benefit.

Pre- and post-training briefings are not tasks to be delegated to the training department. It is a managerial decision to ask someone to attend a training event and it is the manager who should explain that decision.

The pre-briefing should not be concerned with administrative details such as travel arrangements. It needs to focus on the purposes of the training and the briefing manager's expectations of what the training will do for the work performance of the participant. The briefing may also usefully touch upon the question of how the effectiveness of the training may subsequently be measured.

Briefing will be more likely to happen where the manager is provided with a short briefing document giving the key facts about the training and providing a few trigger questions to structure the dialogue with the participant. Sample questions for briefing and de-briefing sessions are given in Figures 4.2 and 4.3.

(Issues and questions to be covered in a typical session of about 20 minutes).

1. What the trainee expects to get out of the training...

2. What the nominating manager hopes to see the trainee get out of the pro-gramme... (the main learning objectives/benefits)

3. What differences the nominating manager thinks the training will make to the way the trainee does his or her job...

4. What will constitute meaningful measures of the benefits realized by successful training...

Figure 4.2 *Manager's briefing of person about to attend a training activity*

De-briefing is all about reinforcing what has been gained during training. The real value of training is not the amount learned on a course but the *use* that is made of that learning back in the workplace. Training activities should not be seen as self-contained happenings that are di-vorced from the real world. Nor should trainees leave a course full of ideas and enthusiasm for doing things better, only to run up against a wall of cynicism or obstruction from their managers, typified by comments such as, 'Had a good holiday?' or, 'Now you can forget all that theory!'.

(Issues and questions to be covered in a typical session of about 20 minutes)

1. What specific, useful things (knowledge/skills) has the trainee gained from the training...

2. How does the trainee intend to make use of new knowledge and skills...
    opportunities to use what has been learned
    action targets
    timetable for completion
    criteria for success

3. What (if any) help does the trainee need in order to make use of what has been learned...
    help from the manager
    help from colleagues or subordinates
    help from trainers
    help with resources (time/money/materials/facilities)

4. What constraints does the trainee anticipate may get in the way of using what has been learned ...

5. When will the trainee and the manager meet to review subsequent progress...

6. What might be appropriate ways for the manager to reinforce changes in the trainee's work behaviours following training...

Figure 4.3 *Manager's debriefing of person following attendance at a training activity*

An effective de-briefing focuses upon what has been learned, either as knowledge or skills, and how this will be applied to the trainee's job. It is not concerned (other than very marginally, say as conversational ice-breakers) with the quality of the residential facilities, the entertainment value of the speakers, or whether the trainee got to that nice little pub in the next village. Effective de-briefing also should discuss the opportunities to do things differently and any constraints perceived by the trainee. The manager has the opportunity to encourage use of new skills and to offer practical support where appropriate.

Over a period of time, the manager can reinforce the training by recognizing and rewarding improved work performance. In due course (timing varies according to the subject matter of the training) the manager can also be involved in an evaluation of the cost-effectiveness of the training. A balance needs to be found between evaluation carried out sufficiently long after the training that the trainee has had time to master and use new skills, but not so long after that the novel elements in working practice can no longer be distinguished with any certainty ('That's the way I normally work').

Usually such evaluation will depend upon the trainers providing a structure and guidance on the appropriate evaluation technique, but nobody is better placed than the manager to carry out direct observation of work performance. The subject of assessing the effectiveness of training is considered in greater detail in Chapter 6.

So far the emphasis has been on the manager's contribution to making training cost-effective, partly because this is the more neglected topic and partly because this book is written primarily for managers. However, managers also need to know what contribution to training effectiveness should be coming out of the right-hand loop in Figure 4.1. We can summarize the positive role that trainers can play in achieving trainer–manager collaboration as follows:

PRACTICAL TIPS

1. Communicate a clearly focused sense of purpose in all training activities.

2. Ensure that all training is seen to be relevant to the work that the trainees do.

3. Build into training continuous action-planning that helps the transfer of learning from the classroom back into the workplace.

These three practical tips are now considered in more detail.

Sense of purpose

The purposes of a training event should always be clear and should be frequently emphasized. Trainers need to create the expectation amongst trainees that what they are learning is something to be used, not just talked about. They should make it clear that training exists in order to improve work performance, in line with corporate strategy, and is not simply rest and recreation.

Sometimes trainers make a big issue of keeping course participants in the dark about what is going to happen to them. They pull managers and people already trained into a conspiracy of silence ('Don't tell people about the course because then you'll spoil it for them...'). This makes pre-course briefing a shadow of what it should be. I would suggest that the practice is not only unethical – people are conned into training events on the basis of incomplete or even misleading information – but plain counter-productive. In my evaluation studies I have come across too many people who are still wondering, months after the training, what the point of it was: that simply adds up to a wasted learning opportunity. When people do not know what the training is trying to achieve, there are two problems: first, they are unable to focus clearly on what they are meant to be learning and may dissipate energy trying to second-guess the intentions of the trainers; second, they may be so preoccupied with their own reactions to the situation itself (frustration, discomfort, anger, etc) that they miss the learning elements contained within the activity.

It is sometimes a valid training activity to create situations that are highly ambiguous or undefined for the learners (so long as those conditions reflect a careful analysis of working conditions and learning needs); but the more ambiguous the nature of the learning experience, the more essential that there is a thorough and open preparation for the activity and an equally thorough de-brief afterwards, undertaken by both the trainers and the participants' managers.

Relevance

The hopes and expectations (and, conversely, the resistances) with which the individual trainee arrives at a training event depend greatly on the extent to which the subject matter is perceived as relevant to that person's own job. Two things increase perceived (and actual) relevance:

- a training design that accurately reflects the substance of the job for which the training is being provided – examples, case studies, exercises, all can be readily identified with by trainees and there is no room for the complaint 'But we do things differently here';
- thorough pre-training briefing, by the trainee's manager (as described above).

Action planning

Throughout a training activity, trainers should emphasize the practical application of learning points ('How does this apply to *your* job?'). It is not remotely adequate, for example, to offer as 'management training' a summary of, say, the better-known management theorists, leaving trainees to make of it what they can. The theory must be translated to show what (if indeed any) direct relevance it has to the way in which the participants perform their particular managerial jobs.

Action planning needs to be an ongoing process, literally session-by-session, and not something crammed into the final hour of a course when people are thinking about their journeys home. This ensures that important points do not get forgotten; it helps trainees to think continually about the applications of what they are learning; and it can lessen the tendency for end-of-event action plans to be empty statements of good intention, written to please the trainers but with no serious expectation that they will be implemented.

Planning for learning transfer needs to be realistic. It recognizes that people can influence their environment and can change their behaviour. It also recognizes that when new ideas and skills need to be applied there may be obstacles to overcome: resources, time, other people's behaviour, entrenched interests, policies and procedures. Techniques such as force-field analysis (which reviews the factors helping and the factors hindering a specific change) provide a helpful framework for breaking free from the log-jam of 'That's a good idea, but...'.

Nevertheless, transfer of learning cannot be guaranteed solely by measures taken within the training activity. The trainee's manager has a key role to play at the de-briefing stage and through subsequent reinforcement and evaluation.

PART 2

Using External Training Resources: (1) Public Courses

Until now, this book has focused on in-house training because that is where the most control over quality can be exercised. Sometimes, though, either the skills are not available within your organization, or the nature of the diagnosed problem is such that you need to make use of specialist external resources – public courses, open learning materials, ready-made video films, or training consultants.

The first point to note is that everything that has been said about in-house training applies with equal force to externally supplied training. If the external training does not relate to the strategic purposes of your organization; if it lacks clearly specified objectives; if there is no evaluation of its effectiveness (an end-of-course 'happy sheet' is *not* adequate!); and if your managers do not reinforce learning after the training, then external training will prove just as ineffective and costly as poorly designed internal training. An external supplier of training may acquire a prestige name either by the quality of the training, or by clever advertising. It is not difficult to distinguish which, before you commit to purchase.

'Have solution, will travel' is a motto that can be applied to a lot of public courses. Inevitably, a public course is pitched at an 'average' participant and it would be remarkable luck to find that all the needs of an individual from a given organization were addressed by any one open event. The cost-effective solution is usually to run the course in-house, provided that it is genuinely adapted to your needs. (Note the comments in Chapter 1 on the subject of 'badge engineering'.) However, where there are only one or two people in-house who have the particular learning need, then a public course may be the only realistic option and a measure of compromise on quality may have to be accepted.

Another consideration with public courses is the experience of the presenters. Many courses are delivered by freelance trainers who are employed simply to deliver that event, using a standard script and materials. This is less of a problem where experienced trainers are used, although even then you may find that the trainer is only as good as the material: in other words, questions that call for depth of knowledge on the subject may lie outside their experience (and the script). Sometimes you will find that a course supplier employs as presenters people chosen for their presentational skills but who have no background in training at all. It is a useful check to ascertain whether or not the person who delivers the course either played a part in its development, or earns a living, independently of their work for that course supplier, by working in that particular area of knowledge or skill.

The activity that follows gives you a checklist for making assessments of external courses, before and after anyone attends them.

ACTIVITY

Checklist for assessing external courses

1. Is it a priority need for your organization?
   - What will the course change?
   - What benefits are specified?
   - If the benefits are attained, what are they worth, relative to the cost of the course?
   - For whom in the organization is this a significant need?
   - What would be a good alternative use of the money?

2. Is the course well-constructed?
- Are the learning objectives stated clearly?
- Is the length of the course appropriate for its purposes?
- Is any pre-course briefing and/or preparation provided?
- Is post-course reinforcement featured?
- Are measures of effectiveness indicated?
- Do the learning methods appear to be appropriate for the subject of the course?
- How will any psychological or physical risks to participants be handled?

3. What are the administrative arrangements?
- Is course information given in plain English?
- Is the location relevant and convenient – or just seductive?
- Is the accommodation satisfactory?
- Is the paperwork clear and informative?

4. What is the reputation of the course and of the supplier?
- Who is actually running the course?
- Did the presenter play a significant part in the design and development of the course?
- What qualifies them for that task?
- What is the track record of the course agency?
- What third-party endorsements can you obtain, independently of the supplier?

5. Have you got options?
- Are there other suppliers?
- Are other suppliers more competent, lower cost, more conveniently located?
- Is there any issue of commercial security involved in attending courses with participants from competitor organizations?
- Could the course be supplied in-house?
- Would an in-house course be better tailored to your needs?
- What would be a per-trainee cost comparison between public and in-house provision?

Using External Training Resources: (2) Open (Distance) Learning

Again, the principles applied to in-house training (and to public courses) apply: diagnose the need, match the solution, reinforce and evaluate. Whilst open learning has been heavily promoted – and is often perceived to be a cheaper alternative to conventional training – these benefits cannot be assumed. Open learning is as good, or bad, as the quality of design work put into it, and critically dependent upon the willingness of learners to make the extra effort. As with any training technique that gets over-hyped (computer-based learning is another case in point) the wrong question is being addressed: the tail (of training technique) is wagging the dog (of learning purpose). Always decide where you want to get to; only then select the medium for training.

Using External Training Resources: (3) Films and Video

Ready-made films are often seen as good value in training, especially when a hire charge of under £100 can be compared to the production cost of a company-specific video of around £20,000 (when made by a professional production house). However, there are several essential questions to ask before using ready-made film material:

• Is it relevant to the training need you are addressing? Film can be a seductive medium; often it *nearly* makes the point you want, but actually deals with something a bit different, or puts it in a context that may be difficult for your people to relate to. Film is also a problem simply because of its visual impact: the quality of the acting may serve to disguise inadequate content; the entertainment factor may overwhelm the learning issues. A form of video that I have found particularly unhelpful is the 'bad example/good example' type; in follow-up studies, I have found that trainees recall the bad examples far more successfully than the good ones, perhaps because they are livelier!

• Is there anything in the film that may undermine its credibility? For example, a film may relate to a different kind of industry, or a different organizational culture. It may be American. It may be dated in appearance (note especially the style of women's clothing), or dated in the attitudes it portrays (conveying stereotyped views of women's roles, for example). Training audiences take a sometimes perverse delight in finding things in films that 'aren't the way we do it here' and use such discoveries to justify rejecting all other messages, however relevant, that the film contains.

• What will people be asked to do in addition to watching the film? Films are too often presented as if the act of viewing them was the whole training process. It should be borne in mind that video tends to be a very passive training medium (not to be used after a heavy lunch!). If it is to work effectively, a video or film needs to be supplemented by activities which involve the viewers, both whilst watching it and afterwards. Two useful techniques are (a) video review sheets which ask questions about key elements of the film – use the answers as a basis for discussion of applications to trainees' jobs; and (b) trigger videos which consist of short episodes interspersed with discussion amongst trainees.

Using External Training Resources: (4) Consultants

Numerous books and pamphlets have been written about the client–consultant relationship, especially the question of how best to choose amongst consultants. A good consultant will offer specialist expertise and a degree of independence which gives greater objectivity when reviewing what is happening in your organization. An effective consultancy assignment has much in common with an effective training design: establishing needs and developing appropriate responses.

The greatest risks of consultancy not working out arise where:

- there is a mismatch of expectations, due to inadequate initial diagnostic work;
- the client has a goal which is being kept from the consultant (clients using consultants to fire their bullets for them);
- the client wants to be seen to be 'doing something', without a commitment to real change;
- where the consultant's diagnosis is too accurate for comfort and the organization closes ranks to protect the status quo;
- where consultants make promises that they cannot deliver, breach confidentiality, or over-charge;
- where the consultancy provides a service that is all presentation and no substance (a particular risk where the supplier employs sales people other than the consultants themselves).

Conclusion

Methods to develop a collaborative working partnership between managers and trainers were presented, the benefit being greatly enhanced effectiveness and value-for-money in training provision. The chapter concluded with a survey of factors contributing to cost-effectiveness when using external training resources: public courses, open (distance) learning, films and video, and consultants.

5 Implementing Effective Training

▷ SUMMARY ◁

This chapter offers practical guidance for the 'part-time' trainer – the line or sales manager who has training as part of their job description – on how to use a number of training techniques either informally, as in the kerbside conference, or as a contributor to more structured training events. These guidelines also provide a set of benchmarks for the manager who needs to review the cost-effectiveness of any training under review.

Introduction

The chapter has been divided into a series of 'Practical Tips', each of which focuses upon an aspect of training competence which is likely at some time to be needed by the manager who is contributing to (or reinforcing) training. At the same time, the guidelines in each section provide clear indicators of what to look for when the manager is reviewing the cost-effectiveness of training provided by others.

Figure 5.1 links each 'Practical Tips' topic to an area of application likely to be of interest to the manager.

TOPIC NUMBER: APPLICATION	1	2	3	4	5	6	7	8	9	10
Kerbside conference							/	?	/	/
Manager training in regular meeting				/	?	?			/	/
Presentation to conference	/		/		?	?				/
Using ready-made video or film	/			/	/	?	?	?		/
Manager opening a training event		/	?							/
Manager as session leader within a training event	/		/	/	?	?	?	?	/	/
Manager reinforcing learning after a training event							?		/	/

Key:
> / – directly applicable
> ? – sometimes applicable

> Topics:
> 1 – Tips on structuring a learning session
> 2 – Tips on opening a training session
> 3 – Tips on training presentations
> 4 – Tips on group discussions
> 5 – Tips on using video with groups
> 6 – Tips on using a case study
> 7 – Tips on interpersonal skills training
> 8 – Tips on running a role play
> 9 – Tips on giving feedback to trainees
> 10 – Tips on encouraging transfer of learning

Figure 5.1 *Applications of 'Practical Tips'*

1. TIPS ON STRUCTURING A LEARNING SESSION

1. It is helpful to adopt a standard format for each session within a training event. This helps you achieve a consistent quality as well as check that no important element of the training design has been missed. A standardized format might resemble the following sequence:

- introductory comments by the trainer, bridging from the previous activity;
- re-statement of the formal learning objective(s) that relate to that session;
- presentation to the audience (information, description and illustration of skills, and so on);
- activity by trainees (questions, discussion, practice of skills, paper-based exercise, and so on);
- connecting learning points to trainees' own work experience;
- summary review of learning points;
- bridging to next session.

2. In similar fashion, a standard format can be adopted for each practical exercise, as follows:

- explanation of 'Why we're doing this exercise';
- description of the steps the participants should follow, including any division of trainees into sub-groups as well as introduction of any support materials (such as behaviour observation checklists – discussed later in this chapter);
- running the exercise (including any interim reviews, correction of errors, etc, as appropriate);
- whole-group ('plenary') de-briefing of the exercise, including preparation by the trainer of trigger questions to provoke debate, reinforce learning and encourage transfer of new knowledge and skills into the trainees' work.

2. TIPS ON OPENING A TRAINING SESSION

1. The opening session sets the tone for what follows. Get housekeeping issues out of the way quickly so that they do not intrude later into the momentum of the event. Housekeeping issues are the administrative details like:

- meal times;
- fire alarms;
- name 'tents' (if you do not know them all personally);
- toilets;
- the time that hotel rooms have to be vacated.

2. After welcoming trainees, get to the point of why they are there:

- state the formal objectives of the event (it is often helpful to have these ready on a prepared flipchart or slide);
- link this event with preceding activities in the organization;
- emphasize your expectation that trainees will learn something useful (they are not here for rest and recreation) – the event is not about theory or good intentions but about practical applications back at work;
- explain how this training event relates to the organization's corporate purposes (this part is not optional!);
- describe how the group will be working – the style of the event, the type of activities, and your own anticipation of lively discussion and active contributions by group members.

3. Invite questions about the broad purpose of the training event, but defer any detailed specifics until the relevant session. This is definitely not the time to start debating what should or should not be included in the timetable.

4. Respond appropriately to anyone who (rightly or wrongly) feels that he or she ought not to be attending this particular event. Depending upon the individual, your response may range from 'Wait and see how the event unfolds before you judge it', through to, 'I agree that you should not be here until you have discussed your learning needs'.

3. TIPS ON TRAINING PRESENTATIONS

1. Aim small: big themes sound impressive but are likely to paralyse initiative ('That problem is too big for me to deal with'). Whatever the performance improvements you are seeking through training, it is worth emphasizing the message that changes come about from hundreds or thousands of small improvements of the kind that your audience can themselves make, rather than from a few great leaps forward.

2. A verbal presentation needs properly developed learning objectives just as much as any other kind of training.

3. A list of key points written onto index cards is easier to work with – and makes your presentation sound more natural – than a fully written-out script.

4. Experienced presenters like to use their own style and choice of words. You can give depth and credibility to your presentation by personalizing it with *relevant* illustrations drawn from your own experience.

5. Remember that slogans and mnemonics, however catchy, do not work; it is the process of applying them to the individual's job that makes the difference. Effective training is that training which helps the trainee to translate the message into practice.

6. When personalizing material, avoid stories that represent a put-down of other people and don't get carried away... your war-stories should be used judiciously and sparsely! They are a supplement to the training content, not the major element in it. When personalizing material be sure that the key learning points do not get omitted or watered down.

7. Beware of humour: it often backfires, either immediately or after the event. Totally avoid jokes about race, colour, religion, politics, ill-health, death, or customers.

8. Your choice of language, tone of voice, body language, all must convey your commitment to the purposes of the training. Sort out any reservations about the training before you get in front of a group. You have to show that you believe in what you're saying.

9. Prepare and rehearse ahead of time. Your credibility is greatly enhanced when you can work without constant reference to notes or prompt cards – though do keep these for emergencies (even the most experienced can dry up sometimes).

10. Watch out for any signs that you may be losing part (or all) of your audience. Be prepared to adjust to differences of experience in your audience. It is helpful to pause every 10 minutes or so to check their understanding and to invite questions.

11. Never forget that the average span of attention is about 20 minutes. Provide frequent changes of activity, eg, from listening to you to discussing how your points apply in their job, or to doing a practical exercise or role play.

12. Merely talking to people is rarely effective: 80 per cent of a lecture is forgotten within 24 hours, unless it is reinforced in ways that involve practical applications.

4. TIPS ON GROUP DISCUSSIONS

1. When you are conducting discussions and need comments from everyone in the group, it is preferable to ask for these in a random order, jumping around the group. Going from person to person, in the order in which people are sitting (aptly called the 'creeping death' approach), often provokes anxiety in those at the end of the line. A random approach also keeps everyone alert since each may be next.

2. When members of a group ask questions, encourage the other participants to respond to this; similarly, when incorrect answers have been given to your own questions, look to group members to correct or expand on the answer. Only supply the answers yourself as a fall-back if no one else volunteers, or if several people have got the answer wrong.

3. Encourage the flow of discussion within the group as much as between individual members and yourself. Not only does this increase group participation and learning (people often learn better from their colleagues than from the person in the training role), it also saves you from the trap of being seen as the only source of information.

4. Group discussion is not (primarily) provided as an opportunity for social chat, nor for theoretical and abstracted discussions of the training topic. On the contrary, use group discussion as a trigger to consideration of the implications of the learning points for the way that participants do their own jobs. 'Knowledge without action is worthless.'

5. Be careful not to get sucked into a fight-to-the-death debate with someone who disagrees with you:

- attack the ideas, not the person;
- remain good humoured;
- broaden the debate so that other group members can respond to that individual.

5. TIPS ON USING VIDEO WITH GROUPS

1. Always make sure that you have watched the film beforehand and made a list of the important learning points that you want people to take away from it.

2. Whenever practicable, run a video in short episodes rather than continuously from beginning to end (some films just do not lend themselves to this treatment – so consider whether they really meet your needs). The point of breaking up the film is to allow you to conduct practical exercises, group discussions and so forth. (It's a good idea to switch off the video and monitor so that there is no distraction during these activities.)

3. Use these intermediate episodes to provoke discussion: ideally, the film will show a mixture of good, bad and middling behaviours in situations to which your audience should be able to relate easily. Note that films which offer a series of 'bad example/good example' pairings can present more problems than they solve, especially if the bad examples are more entertaining than the good.

4. As well as breaking up a film into episodes, it is advisable to give people something to do whilst they are watching it. Video is a very passive medium, so provide a checklist of questions based upon the main learning points in the film. This gives the viewers a focus and also increases the amount that they remember from the film. An example of a checklist, developed in conjunction with a video on customer service skills, follows.

CHECKLIST

Example of a video review sheet for use whilst watching a film

What is the customer in the first episode annoyed about?

If Jane had not retrieved the situation, how many different groups of people with whom that customer is likely to have contact might have got to hear about the organization's error?

What is a customer worth to your organization over a typical life-span?

List five things that Jane did correctly in response to the situation...

List three good things that Bob does to resolve Mr Gray's problems...

List as many things as you can think of that are done badly by the angry clerk in the final scene...

6. TIPS ON USING A CASE STUDY

1. Case studies are a useful training tool to assist people to learn about the *process* of problem-solving; whether or not people get to the 'right' answer is neither here nor there.

2. The strengths of case study as a training technique are that it enables people to identify hidden elements of the problem-solving process and to practise problem-solving skills, in particular:

- to recognize (and challenge) unquestioned assumptions, values and attitudes in the parties to the process;
- to analyse the available information and draw out conclusions and implications from the facts;
- to arrive – by one means or another – at decisions.

3. The role of the manager/trainer who is using case studies has four aspects to it:

- to select (or write) appropriate case studies;

- to introduce the case, setting out the reasons for the trainees to work on the case, and emphasizing the importance of their reflecting upon the processes as these unfold;
- to chart processes (usually, in private notes to provide for subsequent de-briefing of the exercise; sometimes to give continuous feedback during the exercise);
- to de-brief the exercise, helping participants to make sense of their experiences, helping them to draw conclusions about effective problem-solving, and providing a final summary.

4. The role of the manager/trainer who is using case studies does not normally include:

- taking the lead within the group discussions;
- solving the problem.

5. Effective de-briefing of case studies should follow a pattern of:

- recapping on the purpose of the exercise;
- using open-ended questions to trigger debate on the ways in which the group(s) tackled the task;
- reminding the group of any occasions where their group process (their interpersonal behaviour) got in the way of the formal (problem-solving) task (also see the section 'Tips on giving feedback' later in this chapter);
- encouraging connections between what happened in the exercise and the 'real world' of the trainees' own jobs;
- summarizing the main learning points.

7. When people are working on case studies (and many other practical exercises in training) it is often desirable to organize them into small groups of five to seven people. The balance is between groups that are too large – so some people never play an active part – and groups that are too small to generate any fruitful interpersonal processes from which people can learn.

8. Effective case studies should be as simple as is adequate for the learning purpose. There is no virtue in complicated case studies with masses of data to be analysed – *unless* that reflects the specific training objectives. The main purpose of a case is to trigger an experience of a process of working in a group to arrive at a solution to a stated problem and a good trigger may be no more than one sentence long.

7. TIPS ON INTERPERSONAL SKILLS TRAINING

1. This is *the* area of training where the task of writing clear learning objectives is most likely to be substituted by the easier, but meaningless, production of statements about 'good attitude'. For detailed guidance on writing training objectives see, for example, Mager.[1]

2. The effort to define the required changes in behavioural terms does pay off: if you can't specify what you want someone to do differently, you can't train them!

3. An invaluable tool for the manager or trainer involved in interpersonal skills training is the 'behaviour observation checklist'. This can be designed for use with any learning application – selling computers, selling hamburgers, conduct of meetings, interviewing skills, supervision, customer service, and so on.

4. An effective behaviour observation checklist has the following features:

- each item of behaviour relates to a training objective;
- each item is observable – not something to be inferred or guessed at;
- the checklist is laid out in such a way that it is easy to use; plus, sometimes,
- each item is illustrated by positive and negative examples.

5. Each behaviour observation checklist must be developed for its specific training application. Examples are shown in Figures 5.2 – 5.4. There are three aspects of interpersonal behaviour that the trainer may choose to focus upon:

- the content of the behaviour – analysing what kinds of behaviour could be observed (eg, helping or obstructive behaviours);
- the achievement of a task – analysing how effectively a task requiring use of interpersonal skills was carried out (eg, did people learn from the presentation; did the group reach a 'good' decision?);
- the qualities of the behaviours demonstrated (analysing each of the behaviours in terms of its duration, frequency, sequence and quality).

This may be used for observation of either one person's behaviour or the behaviour of a group of trainees.

BEHAVIOUR CATEGORIES	FREQUENCY OF OCCURRENCE (PER 15 MINUTE OBSERVATION PERIODS)			
	0-15	16-30	31-45	46-60
Listening	//	////	/	///
Giving information	### ///	///	//	////
Making proposals	### ////	###	///	// //
Arguing against others' proposals	//	///	////	### //

Figure 5.2 *Frequency analysis within time periods*

6. Where complex behaviours are to be observed, trained observers are necessary; group activities may require several. As a guideline, one trained observer should manage to track three to five trainees displaying six to eight categories of behaviour.

7. Behaviour observation data show whether or not people can perform the skills which the training has tried to impart. A pre-training observation, as well as one post-training, is essential if you want to link learning gain to the training activity so as to demonstrate cost-effectiveness. The data relating to an individual can also be used for personal feedback.

This checklist is useful as a first-stage instrument where a number of behaviour categories (defined from learning objectives) require assessment. The observer writes in relevant examples of the behaviours as they occur, including bad as well as good instances. Write-in observations of this kind provide a basis for more formalized checklists such as the one shown in Figure 5.4.

TELEPHONE USE TRAINING VALIDATION	Is the behaviour present? Y/N?	Brief description of the behaviour observed. Comments on the quality of performance
Behaviour drawn from learning objectives		
Greets caller		
Establishes the purpose of the call		
Chooses appropriate language		
Uses courteous tone of voice		
Handles complaints constructively		
Provides information that customer needs		
Closes call well		

Observer: Trainee: Date:

Figure 5.3 Simple 'write-in' instrument

TELEPHONE USE TRAINING VALIDATION   Observer: Trainee: Date:

Behaviour categories	Examples of Relevant Behaviour (circle instances observed)	
	POSITIVE EXAMPLES	NEGATIVE EXAMPLES
Greets caller	Uses caller's surname. Identifies self. Uses good morning (etc).	Omits caller's/own name. Uses caller's first name.
Establishes the purpose of the call	Asks open and probing questions. Gives verbal summary of purpose.	No clear purpose. Waffles. Fails to gather information needed. No summary.
Chooses appropriate language	No jargon, company abbreviations, or technical terms. Does not talk down.	Confusing use of jargon etc. Use of emotive words. Patronising tone.
Uses courteous tone of voice	Clear. Interesting tone. Varies pace. Conveys warmth.	Mumbles. Monotonous tone. Speaks too fast. Sounds coldly bureaucratic. Aggressive.
Handles complaints constructively	Listens carefully. Gives summary. Involves customer in solution. Proposes actions.	Becomes defensive/aggressive. Argues the facts. No solution proposed.
Provides information that customer needs	Checks need. Gives information clearly. Is accurate. Clarifies if necessary.	Misunderstands need. Inaccurate. Unclear. Ignores/mishandles questions.
Closes call well	Thanks caller. Summarizes conversation.	Abrupt close. No summary of action.

Figure 5.4 *Comprehensive behaviour observation instrument*

8. TIPS ON RUNNING A ROLE PLAY

1. Role play can be a useful means of practising interpersonal skills, although the technique usually works better with classroom training than training in the workplace. At work, role play can seem very artificial and the trainee singled out to take part is more likely to be embarrassed by the exercise. Where everyone is a learner, the method is usually quite acceptable. However, role play may very usefully be introduced in conjunction with video where this is used for short informal training sessions in the workplace. It enables people to practise skills that the video has demonstrated.

2. Much of the value of the method comes from providing structured feedback to the role player. Such feedback should be concerned with how well the appropriate behaviours have been used, not with the person's acting ability. It is often helpful to undertake role plays in threesomes – two people being the main parties in the fictitious action and the third being the observer.

3. The value of the observer's feedback is enhanced if he or she uses a behaviour observation checklist during the role play. This increases the learning for all three; it also ensures the correct behaviours are reinforced, rather than whatever subjective judgements the observer is inclined to come up with.

4. As with case studies, the design of role play briefs should be kept as simple as possible. Role players should *be themselves* within the prescribed situation – it is their real feelings and behaviour that matter. Playing at being someone else simply distances the experience and reduces the scope for learning to take place.

9. TIPS ON GIVING FEEDBACK TO TRAINEES

1. Feedback should help the learner, not serve as an excuse for the manager or trainer to let off steam; reinforcement of good practices through praise is even more important than correction of errors and a realistic balance of positive and negative comments is desirable.

2. Feedback should be given as soon as possible after the observed behaviour has occurred. The duration of feedback should be limited: make the most important points and then stop. Otherwise, the trainee starts to feel ground down.

3. Comments need to be specific, rooted in the detail of observed behaviour, communicated in plain English, and making judgements solely against criteria that had previously been set for the activity.

4. Facts and opinions must be distinguished clearly.

5. The person giving feedback should invite suggestions from the trainee about how improvements might be made.

6. The most effective order in which to deal with feedback, or de-briefing, after training exercises is the sequence:

- the views of the trainee;
- the views of the other role player;
- the views of the observer;
- (only if necessary) the views of the trainer – mainly to summarize and provide balance in the comments.

7. Resistance to feedback can be expected in some instances. It is usually a sign that the comments are accurate but uncomfortable; however, it can sometimes be the case that the resistance is justified because the comments are misguided or reflect poor observation. Do not react to resistance as if it were a personal attack on you, the trainer/manager, nor on the observer. Try to get the trainee to talk about the feelings of resistance themselves, rather than the subject matter of the exercise.

10. TIPS ON ENCOURAGING TRANSFER OF LEARNING

1. You can never take it for granted that, just because someone appears to have learned something on a course, the trainee will make the necessary connections and effort to put it into practice. Furthermore, it is unlikely that any individual will transform the operations of the organization as a whole; but when a number of people all start to make small improvements in the way things are done, the cumulative impact soon becomes apparent. It is therefore essential to cost-effective training that the process does not stop as people go out of the classroom door.

2. Brief people before training so that they know what pay-offs their manager expects them to get from the training.

3. Make action planning an ongoing process, not something crammed into the final hour of a course, when people are thinking about their journeys home. Doing it session-by-session ensures that important points do not get forgotten; it helps trainees to think continually about the applications of what they are learning; and it can lessen the tendency for end-of-event action plans to be empty statements of good intention, written to please the trainers but with no serious expectation that they will be implemented.

4. The learning activities can be designed so that each element is linked to a question about 'How does this apply to my job?' For instance, using the example of a performance standard:

> (A) Each individual work task shall be delivered onwards on the basis of 'right first time'.
> How do I see this applying to my work:…

5. Another way of structuring the question, 'How does that apply to my job?' is to use a set of questions, such as those in the following checklists.

CHECKLISTS

Examples of checklists for transfer of learning from training room to workplace

EXAMPLE I

1. Do we currently do things in that way?

2. Is it effective? (Does it get results?)

3. Is it efficient? (Is it the best way?)

4. How do I know? (What is the hard evidence for my answers to 2 and 3?)

5. Are changes needed:
   - in knowledge or skills?
   - in policies or procedures?

6. What information do I need before I can take action?

EXAMPLE II

1. From this learning event (or, session), what do I most want to:
   - put to use as soon as possible?
   - get more diagnostic information about?
   - get external help for?

2. How do my action points connect with corporate purposes?

3. What training may be needed?

4. What management actions may be needed?

5. What procedural changes may be needed?

6. Who will do what, when?

6. Finally, de-brief returning trainees to check out what they have learned. Action planning notes or checklists used within the training can provide a ready-made framework for such discussions. Agree a timetable for putting these skills or knowledge into practice. This means allowing them do things differently and sometimes to take risks. Managers then must provide constructive feedback on their performance when they try out their new knowledge and skills. Managers can also help by acting as a model for effective behaviour and as a guiding mentor and coach.

7. Planning for learning transfer needs to be realistic. It recognizes that people can influence their environment and can change their behaviour. It also recognizes that when new ideas and skills need to be applied there may be obstacles to overcome: resources, time, other people's behaviour, entrenched interests, policies and procedures. Techniques such as force-field analysis (which reviews the factors helping and the factors hindering a specific change) provide a helpful framework for breaking free from the log-jam of 'That's a good idea, but...'.

Note

1. For a full discussion of writing behavioural objectives, the reader is recommended to consult the works of Robert Mager such as *Preparing Instructional Objectives* (2nd edn, 1991, Kogan Page, London).

6 Measuring Training Results

▷   SUMMARY   ◁

This chapter is concerned with the measurement of training effectiveness in terms both of its impact on work behaviour and on profitability. The inadequacy of end-of-course 'happy sheets' is described. Guidance is offered on the creation of an organizational framework that will support systematic assessment of training effectiveness.

The range of techniques available for measuring effectiveness is outlined and the timing of training assessments is discussed. An Appendix to the chapter offers several outline structures for workshops to assist with learning the skills of measuring training effectiveness.

Introduction

This book is about cost-effective training. Cost-effectiveness implies two kinds of measurement – judgements about *effectiveness* (eg, 'Did the training do what we intended?') and judgements about *value-for-money* (eg, 'Were the outcomes from the training worth the money, time and effort that went into it?'). This chapter will help you to form more systematic assessments about the cost-effectiveness of training than can ever be obtained from the 'happy sheet' data that most organizations mistakenly put up with. After all, if you cannot measure the results that you are getting from training, why spend money and energy on providing it? You are left with nothing more than a blind faith, or hope, that 'it might be doing some good – and probably isn't doing any harm', when neither assumption is in fact justified.

This chapter is concerned with a specialist area of training known as 'validation and evaluation', which addresses precisely these questions of effectiveness and efficiency. Like Chapter 5, this chapter makes comparatively rigorous demands upon the managerial reader but I believe these demands are justified; it is important that non-trainers fully grasp what is involved in assessing cost-effectiveness.

The interest of non-trainers in assessing training effectiveness is made all the more urgent by the long-standing tendency for professional trainers to resist assessment of training, often using the rationalization that the process is too difficult or the data too unreliable. This has been exacerbated by academic analyses of evaluation which endow the subject with a complexity and mystique that seems designed to discourage day-to-day usage in organizations.

Even where some effort is made to obtain feedback on the effectiveness of training, much of what passes for evaluation can be summed up in the weary question, 'What did you think of that course?' Often, too, there is a tendency to see evaluation as a toolbox of techniques – questionnaire, interview and the like – for assessing training in isolation from its context.

Yet evaluation carried through in a systematic way, using appropriate techniques, not only provides an excellent quality control mechanism within training, but also triggers important questions about the role of training in the organization, the part that managers themselves can play in training and the relationship between training provision and corporate purposes. Not least, it enables you to look at the key question of whether internal or external training is providing value for money.

For both managers and trainers within organizations, there are two central concerns about all forms of training. These concerns are relevant whether the focus is upon shop-floor or clerical level, upon management development, or upon board-level learning about new trends and concepts. Those two concerns are effectiveness and value and they can be summed up in three questions which comprise the core of training evaluation.

1. Has the training achieved what was intended?
2. Is what was achieved worth the resources invested?
3. Is there a better way of getting these results?

Why 'Happy Sheets' do not Assess Training Adequately

The most commonly encountered form of training assessment is the end-of-course feedback questionnaire or 'reactionnaire', known more perjoratively as the 'happy sheet'. A well-designed reactionnaire *will* yield some moderately useful though fairly rough-and ready information to trainers, drawing on trainees' perceptions rather than on objectively verifiable data:

- how trainees felt about the course;
- whether particular learning methods were well-received or not;
- whether or not the trainers were perceived to 'perform' well;
- whether the event was perceived to match expectations or formally stated objectives;
- whether housekeeping arrangements were satisfactory.

However, a happy sheet has major limitations, the most significant being that:

- it does not measure learning – at most it gives an indication of whether or not trainees *think* that they have learned something; this self-perception of learning is often very unreliable;
- it provides no information on whether or not learning will transfer into the workplace – what trainees say they will do on happy sheets and what actually happens may diverge widely;
- it does not reliably assess the effectiveness of the training methods, nor that of the trainers themselves; trainees can rarely make useful judgements about the appropriateness of the training methods, and judgements about trainer performance are far too easily swayed by personal feelings (positive or negative) that do not determine the amount of learning achieved.

Happy sheets are not improved by being subjected to statistical analysis, nor by dressing them up in computerized formats. There is no value in a detailed statistical analysis of data that are themselves unreliable and the phrase 'garbage in, garbage out' might well have been invented for end-of-course reviews!

As well as misleading and inadequate data, happy sheets pose another threat to cost-effective training. It is a form of Gresham's Law (which states that bad currency drives out good). Because happy sheets are used so widely, they are often thought of as the *only* method for assessing training, rather than as the *least effective* method. In consequence, opportunities to make proper assessments are lost. Going through the motions with a happy sheet promotes cynicism amongst both trainers and trainees. It contributes to low expectations about training throughout the organization.

Creating the Organizational Framework for Systematic Assessment of Training Effectiveness

To introduce measures of the cost-effectiveness of training is a form of culture change, just as much as are programmes to change management style or to introduce 'quality'. As with all organizational change, there is a lot of inertia to overcome. However, making change by careful evolutionary steps, rather than going for the revolutionary gesture, is not the same thing as finding excuses for inaction. 'That sounds a good idea, but...'.

Strategy and evaluation in training are complementary and inseparable. Making change happen is partly a matter of getting your goals in clear view and partly a matter of such political skills as persuasion, influence and the ability to build alliances. The manager or trainer undertaking evaluation of training is often working as a catalyst of change and this requires a number of key skills:

- entry skills that enable you to get access to the people who have the information you need or whom you need to influence;
- developing relationships – establishing rapport with people, understanding their points of view and needs;
- diagnostic abilities that enable you to analyse the situation, especially the skills of active listening and unbiased questioning;
- getting commitments to action and generating resources;
- providing constructive feedback to those involved.

From the Vicious to the Benign Spiral

Training in an organization can become trapped in a cycle of poor resourcing-> weak design-> resistance to evaluation-> low credibility, which may become a spiral of decline which only resolves itself when the training department is disbanded.

The benign spiral reverses this trend. Systematic evaluation builds up the credibility of training. Positive findings demonstrate that training investment is paying off. Negative findings show that trainers are serious in their intention to increase the effectiveness of training. A measure of honesty about previous performance, combined with a clear intention to do better, is a far more credible position from which to seek support from the rest of the organization, than a pretence that nothing requires changing or improving.

The problem is to break the self-reinforcing pattern of the vicious circle. Systematic evaluation is a powerful tool for the job, which may be reinforced at the start by the use of an external consultant who can bring fresh ideas to bear on a static, taken-for-granted situation.

Learning Validation and Evaluation Skills

It is outside the scope of this book to provide a detailed description of the various techniques that can be used in assessing training effectiveness but this information is readily available.[1]

Two processes need to occur in parallel: the people who will make assessments of training effectiveness must become skilled in their use; at the same time, changes are often needed at a policy level to ensure that evaluation is valued and given positive encouragement. Outline structures for workshops for managers and for trainers are provided in the Appendix to this chapter.

Formal responsibility for measuring training effectiveness needs to be clear. You need to establish who will design evaluation materials, who will gather data and analyse them, and who will act on the findings. It is also necessary to plan for the resourcing implications: it is unrealistic to imagine that trainers can conduct evaluation studies as well as maintain their existing contact hours, preparation time, and so on.

Evaluation within the Training Cycle

In Chapter 3, Figure 3.4, I showed how the training cycle is completed only when evaluation is included. For convenience that figure is reproduced here. It shows the kinds of evaluation question that can be asked in respect of each stage of the training cycle.

The first point to note is that the value of what you find out by using evaluation is very dependent upon two factors in particular:

1. well-designed training objectives, and
2. use of an *appropriate* evaluation technique.

If the learning objectives were fuzzy, so will be your evaluation findings. When people return from a training event saying things like, 'Great event', 'Really enjoyed it', 'Feel I learned a lot', then the warning bells should ring. Clear objectives produce specific outcomes: 'What I can now do differently is...'.

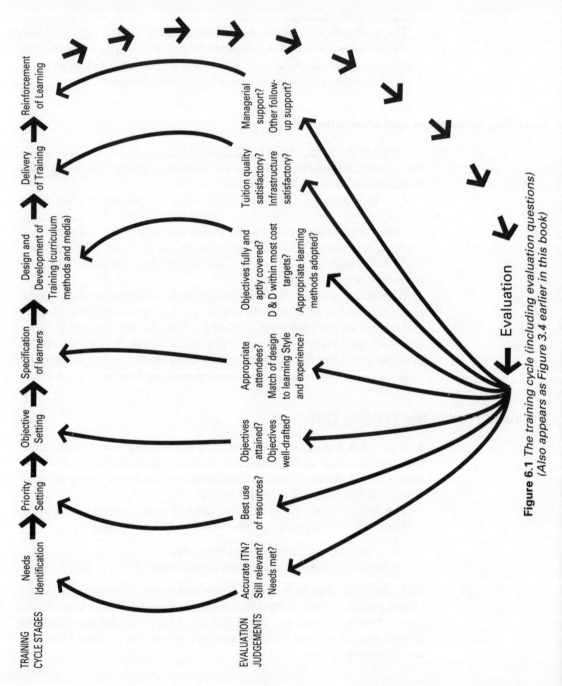

Figure 6.1 *The training cycle (including evaluation questions)*
(Also appears as Figure 3.4 earlier in this book)

Starting to Measure Training Effectiveness

Systematic evaluation of training is more likely to take root where effort is concentrated rather than spread thinly. It is less likely to succeed where token appraisals are undertaken within an organizational culture that is essentially unchanged.

It is futile to try to introduce measurement of training in the face of hostility or 'active apathy'. People take time to absorb new ideas. It is a sound principle to build on strengths and to concentrate initial efforts at evaluation where people are most receptive and the pay-offs are likely to be greatest. 'Ownership' of evaluation projects is important. In the early stages, it is better that people work on the evaluation of training activities for which they personally have some responsibility.

There is also much to be said for concentrating on forthcoming, rather than well-established programmes. In particular, people are more likely to treat evaluation in a spirit of enquiry than one of defensiveness about the status quo. On the other hand, the worth of evaluation can sometimes be established from the impact created by a review that demonstrates that an existing programme is of little value.

There are some rules of thumb for deciding your priorities for assessing training effectiveness. These criteria are:

- *Importance*: how serious would the consequences be if the training failed to work? (Incidentally, this question is also helpful in sorting out the difference between essential and 'nice-to-know' training.)
- *Frequency*: how often will the activity take place? Will the data arrive too late to be used to modify the activity? If it is a one-off event, will the data apply to other events?
- *Cost*: the comparison between the costs of the training activity (and the potential loss if the training is faulty) and the costs of carrying out an evaluation.
- *Impact*: this is a 'political' criterion. Will this assessment trigger worthwhile changes?

Remember too that people in organizations do the things which they are rewarded for doing. The commitment of senior policy-makers to training strategy and evaluation is worth having, but it is many times more useful if that formal commitment translates into influence and rewards that encourage middle and junior managers to play an active role in the training partnership (as described in Chapter 3). A key role in assessing training effectiveness – which only line managers are in a position to undertake – is that of assessing the effects of training on performance *at work*.

For the manager interested in the cost-effectiveness of training, the most important questions will usually concern this impact of training upon work performance, relative to the costs of that training. In order to arrive at such judgements, it is necessary to know something about how different kinds of training need to be assessed by different evaluation techniques.

Techniques Available for Measuring Effectiveness of Training

When it comes to choosing techniques, there are several criteria to guide you. First, and most important, is aptness for the purpose – the correct match between the type of training (eg, knowledge, skills) and the technique. This is summarized in Figure 6.2.

TRAINING SUBJECT	MEASUREMENT TECHNIQUES
Knowledge of facts	Written test
Application of knowledge and use of procedures	Practical test Behaviour observation Action plan Interview Questionnaire
Interpersonal skills	Behaviour observation Critical incident method Repertory grid
Technical (manual) skills Commercial skills	Practical tests
Any type of training	Cost-benefit analysis
Subjective feelings of the learner	Reactionnaire Interview

Figure 6.2 *Types of training subject and measurement techniques*

To take the example of technical skills training, a practical test is normally the appropriate means; to assess an interpersonal skill, some form of behaviour observation. Conversely, it would not be the best choice if, say, a written test were employed to assess interpersonal behaviour.

A second criterion is whether the person using the technique has the skills and experience to use it effectively. This question is of particular concern whenever assessments call for a skill that is superficially similar to, but not in fact the same as, a skill used in other kinds of managerial, personnel or training work. A case in point is that the ability to conduct an effective job selection interview is not a reliable indicator of ability to conduct a non-directive training evaluation interview.

Any evaluation technique needs to be sensitive to the culture of the organization. It must be acceptable to and understandable by the people who experience it. There may be occasions when interview or verbal test has to be used, simply because of respondents' illiteracy. Sometimes, a pictorial method of conveying test information may have to be substituted for a word-based test because of language barriers.

A final criterion is that of secondary benefits from particular techniques. For example, pre-testing of trainees can act as an aid to diagnosing learning-needs analysis. Use of action-plan review as an assessment method also gives a boost to transfer of learning.

Overview of Measurement Techniques

Questionnaire

Questionnaire is the choice of method when large numbers of people need to be surveyed and when the questions that you want to ask will readily allow a closed format, yes/no or multiple-choice response. Questionnaire allows you to ask more (though simpler) questions than, say, interview, but generally produces lower rates of returned documents. It is not a good medium when you want to obtain extended answers from people or to discuss their understanding of issues relating to the training.

Interview

Interview is the ideal method where explanation of actions and decisions is needed, where you need to explore subjects' thought processes, or where the kinds of answer you get are likely to be open-ended. It is helpful where the kinds of answer cannot be accurately anticipated, so that the interview is in the nature of a 'fishing expedition' to identify responses that may subsequently be incorporated into a questionnaire.

The interview should be based upon a prepared schedule of open-ended questions, and typically permit improvised follow-up questions to explore trainees' responses in more depth or to clarify what has been said. Interviews are usually recorded by the interviewer either in writing or by tape-recording. It should be noted that the interview itself and subsequent data analysis are very time-consuming. As a rule, therefore, the technique is limited to small numbers of subjects.

Subject: Interviewing Skills Course

Interviewer................. Interviewee..................

Date...............

Introduction: Greeting and ice-breaking.

Purpose of the interview.

Written or taped record.

1. Please think back to before you attended the course. What did you expect to get out of the course?
2. Looking back, what, if anything, did you actually get out of it?
3. Did you draw up any kind of plan – either on paper or just in your own mind – to put into practice things that you had learned on the course? (Probe for details.)
4. Do you now do anything differently in your work as a result of the course?
5. Is there anything that you would like to do differently but you feel unable to put it into practice? (If yes, probe for details and explanation).
6. During the course, did you find the role plays a useful way of learning?
7. Do you have any comments you'd like to make about the style and methods of the course tutors?
8. Is there anything else that you would like to say about the course?

Close: thank interviewee.

Figure 6.3 *Example of interview schedule for assessing training*

Critical incident review

This self-report technique asks people to complete a regular diary of 'critical incidents' for subsequent analysis. The diary records their direct observations of their own workplace behaviour at moments throughout the day that they themselves consider to be significant ('critical') in the performance of their job roles.

Typical instances include assessing the effectiveness of supervisor training or interviewing skills – indeed, anywhere that direct observation would be unreasonably intrusive. When used properly, the strength of the technique is that it puts behavioural substance into such statements as 'That was a fantastic course!'.

The length of time during which the diary needs to be completed will depend on the nature of the job, that is, upon how frequently 'critical incidents' occur. The diary data is reviewed for evidence of any connections between the training objectives and observable job behaviours described in the diary.

CRITICAL INCIDENT DIARY   Date:.........   Sheet No.........

Please complete one diary sheet for each time that you have to handle a situation that is significant in terms of how effectively you do your job. Include both times when things went well and times when they were less satisfactorily handled.

* * * * * * * * * * * * * * * * * *

1. Give a short factual description of what happened. (Who was involved? What was said and/or done? How long did it all take? What was the outcome?) ——————————————————

2. Was the outcome satisfactory? Very satisfactory/partly satisfactory/ unsatisfactory (*circle one*).
3. Describe what it was that made the outcome more or less satisfactory. ——————————————————

4. Describe briefly any training you have received which you feel has helped you to deal with this particular incident. What difference has the training made? ——————————————————

5. Please mention any lack of training (or inadequate training you have experienced) which you feel has made it more difficult for you to handle the situation. ——————————————————

Figure 6.4 *Example of critical incident diary for assessing training*

Repertory Grid

This technique identifies the behaviours that subjects perceive as correlates of effective and ineffective performance. The technique is complicated, time-consuming and occasionally provokes hostility, although it can give interesting results not readily available by other means. It does not measure actual changes in how people work but merely changes in perceptions. Although attitude change *may* lead to behaviour change, the connection is not automatic. It is generally preferable to use behaviour observation techniques to evaluate what actual change has occurred as a result of training.

Subject: Distinguishing features of...............*trainers*........							
Description of *one* behaviour typical of the pair, but not of the third	Six examples of.....*trainers*.... that I am acquainted with.						Description of one behaviour typical of the third, but not of the pair
	A	B	C	D	E	F	
Prepare very thoroughly	*	*	*				Flies by seat of pants
Answer quest-ions fully	*		*	*			Pokes fun at questioners
					*	*	*	

Overall Ranking

Figure 6.5 *Example of repertory grid form for assessing training (extract only)*

Action Plan Review

The use of action plan review to measure the results of training is akin to the use of critical incident method. It provides an assessment of what trained persons have done differently in their jobs as a result of the training and as written down in a formalized plan for applying that training to their work.

Like all self-report techniques, there is the risk of self-interested responses. However, it is usually quite straightforward to verify whether or not judgements that action plans have been successfully implemented are grounded in reality. The method can be usefully linked with the cost-benefit analysis technique whenever action plans have led to specific projects that have had an impact on work performance.

Action plan review may be combined with follow-up sessions that are a part of the training itself and this, together with the comparatively simple 'action project' focus, makes this a relatively low-cost technique.

---

1. Completion Items consist of (a) an unfinished statement requiring a word or short phrase to complete it; (b) a statement with one or two significant words omitted; or (c) a presentation of information from which the answer may be deduced. Examples:

(i) The meaning of a traffic light when it shows an amber light is...
(ii) A training objective comprises three elements – the ...., the conditions under which it will be performed, and the ....

2. Short Answer Items require answers that are one or two sentences in length. Examples:

(i) Summarize the three main elements that make up a well-drafted training objective.
(ii) What does each of the following initials stand for?

ISE...
IFA...
E&OE...
FIMBRA...

3. Multiple Choice Items require the trainee to identify the correct answer from amongst (usually) three to five plausible alternatives. Example:

When a person is preparing for a new job role, the most appropriate training method to use is (tick one):

action learning
sensitivity training
role play
group discussion

4. True/False Questions are, in effect, a two-option multiple choice question; the fewer the options, the easier it is to get the answer right by choosing at random.

Figure 6.6 *Examples of written test items for assessing training*

Written test

These tests assess changes in factual knowledge. They provide an objective measure of whether trainees can restate what they have been taught. However, where use of knowledge (such as applying a procedure) needs to be tested, a practical test is preferable to a written one. Similarly, whenever interpersonal skills have to be tested, written tests can only be a poor substitute for behaviour observation methods.

Tests can easily be administered to a large group of trainees simultaneously. They are relatively inexpensive to develop and easy to implement, and they yield precise measurement data if used properly.

Practical test

This is the appropriate technique wherever trainees must apply procedural knowledge and manual skills. Practical tests may focus upon the finished task ('Did they make a good widget?') or upon the process ('Did they do things in the right order and also observe safety precautions?').

The cost of practical testing varies considerably, being greatest where test equipment is needed to simulate the operations and faults of machinery.

---

1. Procedure tests. Examples:
   (i)   Describe the correct procedure for removing a car wheel.
  (ii)   Re-assemble this water pump.
 (iii)   Demonstrate what you do with a new life insurance proposal form.
  (iv)   Print out, in date order, all purchase orders received from XYZ Ltd since 1 January 1992.
   (v)   Make the entries to find out which flights have seats available from Amsterdam to London early on the morning of 17 October. Print out the result.

2. Decision-making tests. Examples:
   (i)   Using the information in the case study provided, apply the algorithm to decide the claim for compensation.
  (ii)   Locate and replace the faulty circuit board.
 (iii)   Given an in-tray comprising company reports, previous correspondence, internal memoranda and telephone messages, prepare an action plan for your next sales call.
  (iv)   Examine the carpentry test piece and state, with reasons, whether or not the quality is to specified standards.

Figure 6.7 *Examples of practical test items for assessing training*

Behaviour observation

Behaviour observation is of course a type of practical test, in which the person trained in some aspect of interpersonal skills (as distinct from the technical or commercial skills which are the focus of practical tests) demonstrates the ability to perform that skill.

The technique provides a method for accurate, systematic observation of verbal and physical behaviour, before, during and after training. Post-training assessment in the workplace is often the most useful application and this of course depends on the involvement of managers or supervisors. Behaviour observation checklists require very careful preparation and trained observers.

The strength of the technique is that it emphasizes observable behaviour and discourages guessing at subjects' attitudes. This give it its objectivity, as well as acting as a reinforcement of behavioural learning objectives.

OBSERVER'S CHECKLIST FOR VALIDATION INTERVIEW PRACTICE		
Use of questions	Frequency of use	Specific examples
Open		
Closed		
Reflective		
Leading		
Use of interviewing behaviours	Frequency of use	Specific examples
Inaccurate listening		
Reflective summarizing		
Use of silence		
Interruption		
Clarification		

Figure 6.8 *Example of behaviour observation checklist for assessing training*

103

Cost-benefit analysis

It is usually easier to calculate the input costs of training (salaries, premises, materials, etc) than the value of outputs (improved work performance contributing to attainment of organizational goals). It is, however, usually worth the effort.

Cost-benefit analyses can be thought of as falling into one of two main types: subjective and objective CBA. A useful, relatively subjective way of focusing upon the value of training is to simply ask the client (manager, trainee, etc) what he or she feels the benefits of the proposed training are worth in cash terms. This is often a good question to ask right back at the initial diagnostic stage: 'If this problem can be solved by training, how much would that be worth to you (or: to your department)?'. This approach immediately puts attention on the job-performance benefits of training and on the worth of these benefits.

A more rigorous method is to identify the actual benefits (the outputs) from training and then to quantify these in monetary terms. This is not always easy; sometimes, indeed, it will be a matter of inference and balance of probability rather than a proven cause-and-effect connection between a change in work behaviour and a bottom-line financial change.

That said, it is also often the case that opportunities to put a money value on training are missed; the excuse that the exercise is difficult and sometimes imprecise is an inadequate reason for not attempting measurement. Indeed, the checklist that appears in Chapter 1, page 21, is a reminder of just one list of workplace problems which cost the organization money – and therefore have a demonstrable cash value as benefits from effective training.

Timing of Training Assessments

If you want to establish that training has made a difference to performance, then you have no alternative but to take measurements *before and after* the training. A post-training measure is never enough. The post-measure is useful if you need an indicator of competence, but it is always possible that the trainee was already competent before the training began.

Generally, a pre-training assessment should take place as soon as practicable before the start of training. This minimizes any effect from other sources of learning such as work experience or colleagues. The timing of post-assessments is more variable. Obviously, an end-of-course test is precisely that. It tells you what the trainees could do at the end of training, but of course yields no data on what use trainees subsequently make of that learning within their jobs.

When measurement moves into the workplace, the timing should then be determined by how quickly you expect the trainees to put their new skills to use. That may range from immediately (as, for example, with telephone skills) through to several months after training (as with some management and professional skills, which will only be evidenced if the appropriate situation arises). If the follow-up study occurs too soon after the training event, people may have had little or no opportunity to practise new skills; too late, and the course learning may have been forgotten unless it has been reinforced through regular practice.

Conclusion

Cost-effectiveness in training is about quality issues – the quality of diagnostics; the specificity of learning objectives; the way the training design is put together to match the particular needs of the learners; the crucial element of managerial reinforcement afterwards. Training can be made cost-effective every time, provided that the guidance detailed throughout this book is followed.

If, in addition, you want to measure the extent of that cost-effectiveness you need to use appropriate evaluation techniques such as those outlined in the present chapter. It is important to remember that effectiveness typically is concerned with getting employees to do their jobs better: that is the direct purpose of the training. Only when that level of effectiveness is achieved is it worth going on to use cost-benefit analysis to review the balance of input costs against output benefits, measured in money terms.

Note

1. Newby, T (1992) *Validating Your Training*, London: Kogan Page.
   Newby, T (1992) *The Training Evaluation Handbook*, Aldershot: Gower.

APPENDIX: Introducing Evaluation into an Organization

The framework outlined below has proved successful in organizations where there are several trainers who can learn evaluation skills as a group. This learning approach can, of course, be adapted to the needs of the individual trainer and training manager.

SKILLS DEVELOPMENT	ORGANIZATIONAL CONTEXT
Initial workshop to open up debate and establish pilot evaluation projects.	Policy measures: – Gaining commitment from policy-makers – Creating or re-focusing a dialogue with functional managers
In-depth acquisition of evaluation skills, especially by trainers responsible for course design.	– Reviewing training strategy – Establishing administrative procedures
Routine practice of systematic evaluation, plus updating of skills as necessary	Leadership: – Active goal-setting – Rewarding evaluation activities – Acting on evaluation results

This Appendix contains training objectives and outline designs for three types of workshop that I have run successfully for a wide range of organizations over the years. The workshops can, of course, be adapted to your specific needs.

- *Workshop 1*: a short introduction to strategy, evaluation and validation ideas.

- *Workshop 2*: evaluation techniques and project implementation (five days over about three months).
- *Workshop 3*: a short workshop for managers on ways that they can contribute' to making training more effective.

Workshop 1: A Short Introduction to Strategy, Evaluation and Validation Ideas

Learning objectives

At the end of the workshop, participants will be able to:

- describe key issues in training strategy, validation and evaluation;
- describe and use a framework for determining what they want to assess;
- select techniques for specific applications;
- prepare a first draft of at least one type of instrument, to a standard that is likely to require additional work before it is suitable for implementation.

Topics

- Why do strategy and evaluation go hand-in-hand?
- What is training strategy about?
- Manager–trainer collaboration.
- Systematic training design.
- Quality assurance in training.
- Catalysing change.
- Evaluation and validation: overview.
- Putting a project together.

Workshop 2: Evaluation Techniques and Project Implementation

Purpose

To introduce personnel and training practitioners to practical methods by which they can assess the effectiveness of training within their organization. The workshop is designed for:

- personnel and training managers;
- experienced and newly appointed trainers;
- line managers with training responsibilities.

Participants should have some direct involvement in training design or delivery to provide the basis – during the term of the workshop – for an individual or team-based project.

The workshop is designed for groups of up to 12 people and it is strongly recommended that the training manager should always participate.

Structure of the evaluation programme

1. An initial two days of tutor input and practical design work.
2. A half-day follow-up 7–10 days later.
3. A one-day follow-up about 8–10 weeks later (timing determined by the timetable of training activities within the company).
4. Telephone support to participants during the project stages.

Content of the programme

1. *Initial workshop*

- Training strategy and effectiveness.
- Purposes and benefits of evaluation/validation.
- A strategy for evaluating training.
- Outline of main techniques.
- Practical work to design an evaluation of current or proposed training.

2. *Follow-up half-day*

- Review of ongoing design work on evaluation projects.
- One-to-one coaching.
- Short presentations to the workshop group.
- Processing evaluation data.

3. *Telephone helpline*

- Enables workshop members to obtain advice or to resolve queries arising from their project work.

4. *Final follow-up day*

- Follows implementation of the data-collection stage of projects.
- Review of progress within each project.
- Reporting and using evaluation findings.
- Planning for completion of projects.
- Planning for future strategy and evaluation activities.

Workshop 3: Managers' Role in Effective Training

Learning objectives

At the end of the workshop, participants will be able to:

- describe the key elements of training strategy;
- review the role of training in contributing to the aims of the organization;
- offer relevant, collaborative support to corporate training activities;
- collect validation and evaluation data in the workplace, using evaluation/validation instruments prepared for them.

Topics

- What is training strategy about?
- Outline of main evaluation/validation techniques.

Index